WHERE HOPE TAKES ROOT

HIS HIGHNESS
THE AGA KHAN

. . .

DEMOCRACY AND PLURALISM
IN AN INTERDEPENDENT WORLD

WHERE HOPE TAKES ROOT

DOUGLAS & MCINTYRE

VANCOUVER/TORONTO/BERKELEY

08 09 10 11 12   5 4 3 2 1

Douglas & McIntyre Ltd.
2323 Quebec Street, Suite 201
Vancouver, British Columbia V5T 4S7
www.douglas-mcintyre.com

Library and Archives Canada Cataloguing in Publication
Aga Khan IV, 1936–
Where hope takes root : democracy and pluralism in an
interdependent world / His Highness the Aga Khan ;
introduction by Adrienne Clarkson.

ISBN 978-1-55365-366-0

1. Democracy. 2. Pluralism (Social sciences) 3. Civil society. I. Title.
HM1271.A43 2008   321.8   C2008-900047-1

Editing by Barbara Pulling
Copy editing by Iva Cheung
Cover design by Peter Cocking
Text design by Naomi MacDougall
"Pluralism Is a Work in Progress," His Highness the Aga Khan
in conversation with Peter Mansbridge, is used by permission
of the Canadian Broadcasting Corporation (CBC)
Printed and bound in Canada by Friesens
Printed on acid-free paper that is forest friendly (100% post-consumer
recycled paper) and has been processed chlorine free.
Distributed in the U.S. by Publishers Group West

We gratefully acknowledge the financial support of the Canada Council for the Arts,
the British Columbia Arts Council, the Province of British Columbia through the Book
Publishing Tax Credit, and the Government of Canada through the Book Publishing
Industry Development Program (BPIDP) for our publishing activities.

CONTENTS

. . .

INTRODUCTION

· · · ·

MY INTEREST IN His Highness the Aga Khan, and in his vision, dates back to 1957. Then, as a young university student, I read about Prince Karim, who had suddenly inherited his grandfather's mantle as the Imam, spiritual leader of the Ismailis. His grandfather had been a remarkable figure of worldwide renown. The young prince was still a student at Harvard, and I remember thinking, "How does he feel about inheriting this enormous responsibility as the leader of the Ismailis at the age of twenty?"

In the early 1970s, I was well aware of the Ismailis who, among other Asians, were fleeing Uganda and of our reception of thousands of them here in Canada. I was always grateful that our country, under the leadership of Pierre Elliott Trudeau, welcomed these people, who had found themselves in an extremely difficult and dangerous situation in the country that they had called home.

When I became governor general of Canada in 1999, I met a number of Ismailis in prominent positions in Ottawa and in Toronto, and later in many of the cities across Canada. But it was not until 2002 that I met His Highness, during one of his visits to Ottawa. Immediately, I was deeply impressed by this soft-spoken man, who had given nearly five decades of his life to bettering society in very practical and meaningful ways. His contributions to education, health and cultural revitalization through architecture and town planning in the developing world were without equal. I was very happy to meet His Highness several more times throughout my years in Ottawa and to participate in the Foundation Ceremony of the Delegation of the Ismaili Imamat in June 2005.

I remember the day of the ceremony well. Tents had been erected over the area where the guests were seated, and flowers had been planted to create a garden atmosphere and a sense of beauty and lightness. In my exchanges with His Highness that day, I felt very much that our country could not have a more useful or meaningful relationship. The Aga Khan understands profoundly what Canada is all about and what a diverse society can accomplish if it is built on awareness of difference and relaxed understanding.

In the speeches collected in *Where Hope Takes Root*, the Aga Khan explains the principles that inform his profound belief that civil society, democracy and mutual understanding must be encouraged and strengthened in order for the world to be a better place.

The Aga Khan is not only a spiritual leader. As Imam, he is responsible both for leading the interpretation of the faith and for helping to improve the quality of life for all in the wider communities in which Ismailis live. This dual obligation is often, I think, quite difficult to appreciate from the Christian viewpoint of the role church leaders are expected to perform. In Islam, the worlds of faith and action, of ethical premise and society, are treated together. The Aga Khan sees his responsibilities as encompassing a strong commitment to the well-being and dignity of all human beings, regardless of faith, origin or gender. The intersection of faith and society has led to initiatives that over the last fifty years have made a profound difference in the developing world. The Aga Khan Development Network has improved the lives of some of the poorest, most deprived and most diverse populations in the world.

The Aga Khan realizes that no effective development can happen without the precondition of a healthy civil society. Only a strong civil society can help sustain real change for both rural populations, which are geographically isolated, and the urban poor, who are similarly marginalized from the social, economic and political life of their wider society.

The second precondition for successful development is something for which the Aga Khan and his development network are now increasingly well known: a commitment to pluralism. The efforts of the Imamat have had a pervasive effect, over the last decade particularly, in making the world understand how society must support people of different backgrounds and interests to organize themselves in diverse institutions for a variety of purposes—all in the context of a creative free expression. Pluralism is as important as human rights in ensuring peace, democracy and a better quality of life.

In these speeches, His Highness points out how the rejection of pluralism has helped to incite hatred and conflict among many cultures, nations and religions. This has occurred in places as varied as Afghanistan, Tajikistan, Rwanda and the Democratic Republic of Congo. These sad examples show us that pluralism is critical to peaceful, harmonious understanding. The Aga Khan understands, too, that pluralism does not happen by accident but is the product of enlightened education, moral and material investment by governments and the recognition by all of our common humanity.

As His Highness recognizes, Canada is very open to these ideas. Eighty per cent of Canadians believe it a good thing that we are a diverse population. In this, we may be unique in the world. It is a happy situation for us to have communities of people who are educated, are confident in their identity in Canada and feel assured of the depth of both their own traditions and those of the people who share their institutions and governmental structures.

In his public utterances, the Aga Khan shows great subtlety of mind. He has been the inspiring founder of universities and colleges, because education is one of the democratic pillars he recognizes. He exhorts people everywhere to train leaders and to shape institutions using the highest standards of excellence. His sensitivity to formal learning alerts us that education is not the promulgation of dogmatic commitment or ideological choices. Instead, as he emphasizes, scientific problem solving must exist side by side with a continued openness to new questions.

Memorably, His Highness asserts that the deplorably fashionable phrase "clash of civilizations" is really a "clash of ignorance." This ignorance is both historical and current, and he is unequivocal in his belief that it could have been avoided through more dialogue and understanding between the Judeo-Christian and Muslim worlds.

I find His Highness's belief in what democracy can do to be most inspiring of all. He understands the need for us to be flexible in supporting the diverse institutions that make up democratic life. He is clear eyed and decisive about the breakdown in democratic institutions such as parliaments, which often lack an efficient structure and human capacities to grapple with complexity. Above all, he understands that democracy can only come about through education and awareness. Finally, His Highness identifies the need to strengthen public integrity as the sound foundation on which democracy can rest. It is not simply governments that make democracy work; the most successful democracies are those in which the non-governmental institutions of a diverse civil society play a vital role.

Again and again, the Aga Khan returns to the need for respect and cooperation between Islamic and Western peoples. The Quran tells us that mankind was created by a single Creator "from a single soul," a powerful affirmation of our common humanity—something that differentiates humans from other forms of life. His Highness also speaks meaningfully about the need to maintain a profound humility before the Divine. With this kind of humility, we can turn away from dogma and approach each other as human beings, meeting on a field of respect without anger, without discrimination and without preconceptions. Humility that will lead us away from self-righteousness and ready-made ideology and open us to genuine religious feeling, in its most positive form.

In these remarkable speeches, the Aga Khan gives us a deep sense of what it is to live a life of spiritual and ethical commitment. Across religious, cultural and racial distinctions, we can all help create a universal ethical sensibility.

The Right Honourable Adrienne Clarkson, PC, CC, CMM, CD
Twenty-sixth Governor General of Canada
November 15, 2007

ENHANCING PLURALISM

KEYNOTE SPEECH CONCLUDING *the*
PRINCE CLAUS FUND'S CONFERENCE *on*
CULTURE *and* DEVELOPMENT

Amsterdam, The Netherlands, September 7, 2002

IT IS WITH gratitude and admiration that I participate in this event today. It gives me the opportunity to express publicly the enormous respect in which I hold Prince Claus and the very great importance I attach to the work of the Prince Claus Fund for Culture and Development.

The founding purpose of the Prince Claus Fund— "expanding insight into cultures and promoting interaction between culture and development"—has been fulfilled by means of a vigorous program of grants, awards and publications. These actions recognize, stimulate and support activities that share the principles of equality, respect and trust and have the highest levels of quality and originality. Through them, the Fund is making a very significant contribution in an area I believe will be critical to the development of humankind in the twenty-first century—the strengthening and enhancement of pluralist civil society, in all corners of the globe. The work the Fund has accomplished has given legitimacy and stimulus to the broadest range of intellectuals, artists and·committed groups and organizations, frequently in areas of the world where the importance of such creativity is not recognized and indeed is often repressed. These initiatives constitute highly creative investments in the identification and premiation of forces working to strengthen and enhance the pluralism of cultures that will provide strength into the future. It is my conviction that strengthening institutions that support pluralism is as critical for the welfare and progress of human society as are alleviating poverty and preventing conflict. In fact, all three are intimately related.

The field of development has yielded more than its share of buzzwords. Phrases like "civil society," "poverty alleviation" and "sustainable development" are familiar to many of you, as is the phrase "enabling environment." I must carry responsibility for that, since it was the Enabling Environment Conference in Nairobi, sponsored by the Aga Khan Development Network, the World Bank and others, that brought that phrase into common use. I hope my remarks might result in some more buzzing, because the essence of what I will say this evening refers to "enhancing pluralism."

I do not think it is necessary to spend time outlining the challenge that the process of globalization represents vis-à-vis the cultural fabric of our world. But the content of the new media is not the real threat, nor even is its domination by media giants. The problem is that large segments of all societies—in the developing world and the developed world—are unaware of the wealth of global cultural resources and, therefore, of the need to preserve the precious value of pluralism in their own and in others' societies. Unfortunately, pluralism has not seen any development that parallels the recent acceptance by international public opinion of the imperative to preserve and enhance our natural environment and the world's cultural heritage as "public goods" worthy of general support.

I would go even further and say that the inability of human society to recognize pluralism as a fundamental value constitutes a real handicap for our development and a serious danger for our future. Since the end of the Cold War, a number of factors appear to have been common and significant ingredients in, if not the primary cause of, many of the conflicts we have witnessed. Perhaps the most common of these ingredients is the failure of those involved to recognize that human society is essentially pluralist. Peace and development require that we seek, by every means possible, to invest in and enhance that pluralism. Groups that seek to standardize, to homogenize or, if you will allow me, to normatize all that and those around them must be actively resisted through countervailing activities.

Whether in Central Europe, the Great Lakes region of Africa or Afghanistan—to cite just one example from three different continents—one of the common denominators has been the attempt by communal groups, be they ethnic, religious or tribal, to impose themselves on others. All such attempts are based on eradicating the cultural basis that provides group identity. Without cultural identity, social cohesion gradually dissolves. Human groups lose their necessary point of reference to relate to each other.

For pluralism to succeed, the general education of the populations involved must be sufficiently complete so that individual groups, defined by ethnicity, religion, language, and the like, understand the potential consequences of actions that might impinge on others. This is, for example, one of the principal reasons why today there is so much uninformed speculation about conflict between the Muslim world and others. For instance, the historical root causes of conflict in the Middle East or in Kashmir are not addressed at any level of general education in the most powerful Western democracies that dominate world affairs.

As a Muslim, I stand in front of you in amazement that the Western world had to experience the revolution in Iran to learn about Shia Islam, or the civil war in Afghanistan to learn about Wahhabi Islam. Please remember that we are talking about a religion that one-fifth of the world's population follows. This ignorance is equivalent to Muslims being unaware of the distinction between Catholics and Protestants within Christianity. The point I wish to make is that the governments, civil societies and peoples of this world will be unable to build strong, pluralist societies with the present level of global cultural ignorance. Even the most developed countries will need a massive effort to educate the world's youth in a more thoughtful, competent and complete manner to prepare them for the global responsibilities they will be expected to fulfill. This education is particularly critical in the increasing number of functioning democracies where an informed public plays such a central role.

The actions to enhance pluralism have to be matched in the developing world by programs to alleviate poverty because, left alone, poverty will provide a context for special interests to pursue their goals in aggressive terms. Urgent humanitarian assistance is indispensable, but it should be part of a long-term strategy of helping the recipient community develop its own resources, resources that can help improve the socio-economic conditions of the poorer segments of the population and provide charitable support for those unable to work.

As you know, development is sustainable only if the beneficiaries become, gradually, the masters of the process. This means that initiatives cannot be contemplated exclusively in terms of economics but must be seen as an integrated program that encompasses social and cultural dimensions. Education and skills training, health and public services, conservation of cultural heritage, infrastructure development, urban planning and rehabilitation, rural development, water and energy management, environmental control and even policy and legislative development are among the various aspects that must be taken into account.

To illustrate this approach, I would like to say something about the work that the Aga Khan Development Network has recently launched in Afghanistan. The scenario is dramatic: a country destroyed by decades of war, lacking basic infrastructure, economic resources and institutional fabric, and suffering from strong, antagonistic social and religious forces. The government must also facilitate the return to the country of hundreds of thousands of displaced families, feed the population, restore agricultural production, provide essential social services, eradicate drug-related crops and their ancillary industries, and last, but most essentially, consolidate a culture of tolerance based on the mutual understanding among peoples of different origins and languages.

In this context, the Aga Khan Development Network has started work in Afghanistan based on an accord signed with the government. In the first phase, the Network's priority will be to respond to the most pressing problems. Activities underway include providing humanitarian aid to address both the food shortage in the country and the needs of hundreds of thousands of displaced people by facilitating the resettlement of refugees and rehabilitating buildings and public works required to provide basic social services.

Simultaneously, planning is underway to help address the country's needs in terms of building human and institutional capacity for social and economic development. The Network is taking steps to revive and update institutions to train teachers and nurses to meet the needs of urban and rural populations. Work is also underway to reform the school curriculum in accordance with the government's guidelines and current international experience and to make basic health services accessible to all. We are establishing a microfinance facility to provide financing for agriculture, micro-enterprise, small business including cultural enterprises, and the special needs of refugees returning to properties that have been destroyed.

In all of this work, the cultural dimension is pivotal, because of the pluralistic nature of Afghan culture and the severe stress it has endured in the recent past. As an initial undertaking, the Aga Khan Trust for Culture is working in Kabul to rehabilitate the historic fabric of the ancient city: its monumental buildings, traditional housing and decayed public spaces. These projects are centred on two significant historic sites: the Mausoleum of Timur Shah, considered by many to be the founder of modern Afghanistan, and the Paradise Garden of Babur, the founder of the Mughal Empire in the Indian subcontinent. The goals range from the lofty—the preservation and restoration of symbolic monuments of Afghan history and cultural identity—to the very practical—immediate employment opportunities and the rebuilding of marketable skills. All of them are essential to enable the people of Afghanistan to rebuild their country in peace and dignity.

I would like to leave you with a final thought and some questions and conclusions that flow from it. Developing support for pluralism does not occur naturally in human society. It is a concept that must be nurtured every day, in every forum—in large and small government and private institutions; in civil society organizations working in the arts, culture and public affairs; in the media; in the law, and in the areas of social justice, such as health, social safety nets and education, and economic justice, such as employment opportunities and access to financial services.

Is it not high time, perhaps even past time, that a systematic effort be undertaken to document "best practices" by looking closely at the array of public policies and structures that support pluralism in particular national settings? As we extract lessons and identify models, should we not put a process in place to share them widely for replication? Should not this effort reach out to as many countries as possible, and in as many organizational and institutional settings as we can mobilize?

In addition, each of us can help enhance pluralism in our personal, professional and institutional domains. We could play our role in favour of pluralism as public-opinion makers. We could participate in and support the efforts of groups and NGOs that promote that cause. We could volunteer our professional competences in a variety of fields: academic, technical or managerial. We could also serve the cause of pluralism simply through tolerance, openness and understanding towards other peoples' cultures, social structures, values and faiths, thereby setting an effective example in our own society.

My hope is that society as a whole will not only accept the fact of its plurality but will undertake, as a solemn responsibility, to preserve and enhance pluralism as one of our fundamental values and an inescapable condition for world peace and further human development.

IS CIVIL SOCIETY BANKABLE?

ANNUAL MEETING *of the* EUROPEAN BANK
for RECONSTRUCTION *and* DEVELOPMENT

Tashkent, Uzbekistan, May 5, 2003

IT IS A particular honour to have been invited to deliver the Jacques de Larosière Lecture to such a distinguished gathering. It is, I must admit, an honour that I accepted with considerable trepidation. My first reaction was to question whether I would have anything to say that would be of interest to this audience. Unlike those who have presented the Larosière Lecture in previous years, I am not an economist, a banker or a specialist in national or international finance.

But I have been involved in the field of development for nearly four decades. This engagement has been grounded in my responsibilities as Imam of the Shia Ismaili community and in Islam's message of the fundamental unity of *din* and *dunia*—spirit and life. Throughout its long history, the Ismaili Imamat has emphasized the importance of activities that reflect the social conscience of Islam, that contribute to the well-being of Allah's greatest creation, humankind, and that reflect the responsibility Islam places on the fortunate and the strong to assist those less fortunate.

When I became Imam in 1957, I was faced with developing a system to meet my responsibilities in an organized, sustainable manner that was suited to the circumstances, demands and opportunities of the second half of the twentieth century. In a period of decolonization in Asia and Africa, the Cold War and its disastrous impact on developing countries, and painful progress towards a global movement for international development, it became essential that the Imamat's economic and social development efforts be broadened beyond the Ismaili community to the societies in which the community lived. Presently, the Ismaili community of approximately 15 million resides in Asia, Africa, the Middle East, Europe and North America.

This aim led me to establish what is now the Aga Khan Development Network (AKDN), a group of agencies with individual mandates, to engage in critical dimensions of development from distinct yet complementary perspectives and the competencies these dimensions require. The Network is active in the fields of health, education, civil society enhancement, culture, and economic and rural development. It now has more than three decades of experience working in South Asia and eastern and western Africa' and since 1993 has been active in Central Asia. This work started in Tajikistan with humanitarian assistance and then post-conflict reconstruction and redevelopment, and it has expanded to other countries, including Kyrgyzstan and Kazakhstan more recently. The Network's newest engagement is a major commitment to reconstruction and development in Afghanistan.

Time and experience have taught us a number of lessons that you may already know but that explain why our development agencies are structured in number and purpose as they are. Development is a multifaceted process that requires approaches from multiple perspectives and competencies; necessitates local communities or beneficiaries to mobilize and develop the capacity to take responsibility for activities designed to produce sustained results, and requires long-term engagement with programs developing into permanent and localized institutions. The structure and operating principles of the Network are a response to this understanding of development. These agencies are all field-based, with a small headquarters staff, and draw on the energies of more than 20,000 employees and volunteers. The long-term perspective and the field-driven experience of the AKDN will be the basis of my remarks this afternoon.

I am sure we can agree that, at the most general level, the goal of all development efforts—be they promoted by governments, national organizations or international development agencies and institutions—is to stimulate and facilitate change that is positive in character, significant in impact, long-lasting in consequence and sustainable into the future. The more complex and difficult question is, what does it take to achieve development that meets this aspiration?

Economic development—increasing the production and consumption of goods and services in the economy and expanding and improving the quality of employment opportunities for a country's population and its disposable income—is certainly critical. I take this goal as a given, and that is why the Aga Khan Development Network has several agencies whose primary objective is to expand economic opportunity in selected sectors. However, the quality of life does not clearly have a direct, one-to-one relationship with the level of production or even the breadth of access to what an economy produces. Without doubt, growth plays a central role in increasing human welfare and dignity. But other dimensions and challenges to development play at least an equally important role.

Unfortunately, many of them are not easily measured in conventional economic terms nor addressed through usual economic programs and policies. It is to these aspects of development that I would like to devote most of the rest of my remarks, for two reasons. The non-economic dimensions of development often escape the attention they deserve, because the degree of risk of *not* doing something is often underestimated. Secondly, when dealt with competently and over time, these non-economic dimensions actually support and sustain the health of the economy as well as other aspects of society.

From the perspective of forty years of work, and the experience of the agencies of the Aga Khan Development Network, institutional development stands out as critically important to broad-based sustainable change. By institutional development, I mean the strengthening and refocussing of existing institutions, as well as the creation of new institutions and policies to support them. Because this process takes time, it is also urgent. Institutional development is essential to respond to emergent needs, new opportunities and persistent gaps if change is to measure up to the standards of being positive, significant, long-lasting and sustainable and having a genuinely measurable impact. No country, to my knowledge, can achieve stable, continuous growth if its civil society is constrained by inherent institutional instability.

The need is universal. It exists in big countries and small countries; countries well endowed with natural resources and those that have less; countries in the developing world and the developed world, including those in transition following the dissolution of the Soviet Union. The need for institutional development also applies to every sector of society: to government at all levels, to business large and small and to that diverse array of informal and formal organizations that have come to be referred to collectively as civil society institutions. One clear lesson of the last half of the twentieth century is that governments cannot do everything. The role of the private business sector in national economies is now universally acknowledged as both critical and legitimate.

But the importance of refocussing existing institutions and developing new ones to enter spheres of social activity previously undertaken solely by government is not yet as widely recognized. Nor is there as clear an understanding of what form new institutions might take or how they should relate to government—an issue that is at least being addressed with respect to government's relations with the private business sector, as opposed to the private social sector. In the latter, lack of clarity, even confusion, dominates the field. What do I mean when I speak of civil society institutions? Of the three sectors—government, private business and civil society—it is the most diverse and the least well understood. Moreover, I am not sure that even those who work in the sector define it in the same way. My purpose is not to enter into an academic discussion but only to ensure that I am understood. I prefer to think of civil society in the widest sense, including all sorts of organizations and initiatives. It includes much more than is captured by the term "NGO." I would, for instance, include professional organizations that aim to uphold best practices or that serve and contribute to a vibrant and effective business sector, such as chambers of commerce, associations of accountants, bankers, doctors and lawyers, and the like.

Civil society organizations are generally non-profit or not-for-profit, at least implicitly. They may, however, generate money from fees or services that they provide. This characteristic is the source of great confusion in many parts of the world, because "non-profit" is frequently confused with "charity"—giving services or sustenance to the needy. The confusion is understandable, because charity has a long history in all religious traditions, and it renders real assistance to those not able to help themselves. Some civil society institutions should and will always be involved in charity. But those of a new type exist to provide services in return for fees that will cover some or all of the costs of operations, including salaries, but not produce a profit for owners or investors. Perhaps "non-commercial" conveys the purpose and operating principles of civil society institutions in many parts of the world more clearly than the term "non-profit." Because most civil society institutions are non-commercial, and whatever dividends they produce contribute directly to improving the quality of life of their beneficiaries, these institutions face the fundamental problem of identifying financial resources that will keep them alive and enable them to grow.

At the heart of the issue is the question "Is civil society bankable?" If so, what criteria should apply? The long history of the AKDN agencies has shown that, although numerous financial institutions and programs are available to support economic investment, non-commercial civil society institutions face the permanent threat of being systematically underfunded. One of the causes, at least from the experience of AKDN, is that civil society institutions are rarely, if ever, part of a national planning process. Relations between public-sector and private-sector health or education delivery, for example, are more often left to chance than being a thought-through process driven by clear development goals. Within the civil society sector, there is not even consultation among the providers working on the same problems from different perspectives as to how they might work together for better effectiveness. In addition, financial institutions find it difficult to rationalize the role, needs and futures of civil society institutions within the national economy. At least in the banking sector, these institutions cannot tailor their financial support systems, when available, to the characteristics of non-commercial civil society institutions. A number of these characteristics are common, such as the need and desire for longevity; the incapability to plan growth on the basis of secure, long-term funding; the need to employ competent people at fair market rates, and in some cases the inability or unwillingness to become a commercial venture.

I would like to share with you some specific examples from our own activities in this region. How does a private-sector hospital that has chosen not to offer its services for commercial gain fund its expansion or the cost of increasingly expensive, sophisticated technical equipment? How does a private university fund its expansion into new areas of higher education when student fees will never reasonably cover more than 25 per cent of the cost of running the university? How do you address the now well-recognized problem of pockets of poverty in developing countries that clearly present a real threat of destabilization but that have no hope of seeing improved economic standards until a key piece of unbankable infrastructure is built? A good example is the recently constructed bridge linking Tajik Badakhshan and Afghan Badakhshan, which could never be justified on the basis of normal banking criteria.

Within civil society in much of the developing world, some professions are critical to stable growth and to democracy but are systematically underresourced in terms of pay and opportunities for ongoing training. The three groups I would cite today are teachers, nurses and journalists. The economic status of these professions simply has to be corrected if the consequences are not going to be the progressive degradation of education, the progressive degradation of health care and the deterioration of the national media, which will be left incompetent or open to all sorts of undesirable pressures, including corruption. And yet the additional costs of better remuneration to such professions will simply add to the end cost of the product, making it even more inaccessible to those who need it most—the poor.

In the developing world, the backlog of unmet existing needs, combined with the needs of rapidly growing populations, puts incredible pressure on even the most forward-looking, well-resourced and efficient governments. In the countries of the former Soviet Union, the previously high levels of achievement in health and all levels of education are no longer sustainable because governments cannot provide the same levels of subsidies. And in all parts of the world, the growing differentiation and specialization in the fields of health and higher education demand institutions of a new type, mastery of new areas of knowledge and technology, the capacity to innovate, and the identification of new sources of funding. Not even the governments of the richest countries in the world can meet these challenges without contributions from the private business and civil society sectors.

Civil society organizations need to reach for the highest level of competence to justify their support. The sector combines energy and creativity with a social conscience. Together, these constitute a powerful impulse and should be nurtured. At the same time, capacities for management, program design and implementation, fundraising, and self-study and evaluation need to be strengthened. Learning from the experiences of the sector is important for the organizations themselves, as well as for government, international development agencies, universities and even the private business sector. How can we improve the process of self-analysis and evaluation and the exchange of experiences without diminishing the autonomy and creative initiative of civil society institutions? How can they learn from their own experiences in order to improve the management of their programs?

The Network's experience also reveals that the civil society sector faces a number of challenges that must be addressed if the sector is going to make an effective, continuing contribution to national development in this region. Even when needs are readily evident, the sector's role and potential are not well understood. Critics question its legitimacy, and no framework, no predictable and reliable environment, exists in which civil society organizations can function and prosper. To whom, and for what, the sector is responsible and accountable are often unclear. And few appreciate how the sector is and can be financed and sustained. How should these civil society institutions be governed? What standards should be applied to define their success?

Governments, donor agencies and others need to do more to create an environment that enables civil society institutions to emerge and develop. The basic issue is how to improve mutual understanding and to create the conditions of confidence and mutual predictability that will enable people and institutions to realize their full potential. Some larger contextual issues are critical as well.

The first of these is regional cooperation, a subject that has been mentioned at various points in the program over the last two days, although primarily in terms of its economic consequences. The last few years have seen the emergence of groups of neighbouring countries coming together to promote trade and broader economic relations. This movement is critically important for Central Asia as well, and it can build on the demography of the region and elements of common culture that have developed over extended periods of time, as symbolized by the Silk Road. Central Asia is still well situated to play an important role between Europe, China and the Indian subcontinent. That role will be more important and have greater impact if the countries of the region can find ways to develop their economies and resources on a cooperative basis, rather than as individual nations. But why restrict this cooperation to the commercial domain? Many civil society needs are clearly regional; hence our creation of the University of Central Asia in partnership with the governments of Kazakhstan, Tajikistan and the Kyrgyz Republic to provide regional education specialized in high mountain studies.

Pluralism is the recognition that people of diverse backgrounds and interests, organizations and projects of different types, and different kinds and forms of creative expression are all valuable and therefore deserving of recognition and support by government and society as a whole. Without support for pluralism, civil society does not function. Pluralism is also essential for peace, a statement that is unfortunately documented by armed conflict in contexts of cultural, ethnic or religious differences on almost every continent at this time. It is of particular importance here in Central Asia, given the demography of most countries.

The purpose of my comments today is not to point an accusing finger at international or national banking systems. Nor do I want to appear ungrateful for the generous assistance we have received from our donor-partners over the last many years. I do want to share with you, however, my deep conviction—drawn from years of experience—that financial support systems for non-commercial civil society institutions do not exist in certain countries, are insufficient or are ill-adapted to the needs of such institutions.

If the international financial community is willing to look in depth at the problems to be addressed in supporting non-commercial civil society institutions, some strategic goals should be set. The first one I would propose to you is to ensure that, as civil society grows, it does so in a manner that enhances public appreciation of the diversity of people within common frontiers as an asset, not a liability. Events in recent years in eastern Europe, in the Great Lakes area of Africa and in numerous countries in Asia, including Afghanistan and Tajikistan, have shown that these societies must develop in such a way that each group within them feels valued and respected and is encouraged to contribute to the goal of national development.

I do not believe that most people are born into an environment where they see pluralism as an asset. However, I am convinced that civil society institutions have a central role to play in bringing value to pluralism and inclusiveness. But again, who will fund the tools with which pluralism will find its way into civil society, as a central necessity for civilized life in the future?

Thank you for hearing me out. I was not invited here to speak to you about banking, although I clearly understand and admire the purpose of the EBRD, which is development through economic stimulation. Creating a sound future for the peoples of Central Asia requires just as much, in my view, a clear focus on building new concepts and new institutions for new civil societies.

THE KNOWLEDGE REVOLUTION
AND THE END OF IGNORANCE

CONVOCATION, AGA KHAN UNIVERSITY

Karachi, Pakistan, December 6, 2003

BISMILLAH-IR-RAHMAN-IR-RAHIM. I share the joy and pride of everyone associated with the achievements of AKU's 241 new graduates. You enter the world as nurses and physicians, researchers and educators, with the University's and my highest expectations that you will contribute to your societies as professional givers of health care and solace, and of educational skills and aspirations, but also as intelligent and wise voices in the communities you serve. This is a time that will call for the very best of truly educated minds: your skills and specialized knowledge, but also your patience and tolerance. Above all, it will call for your understanding. May you bring reason and hope to all whom you touch in your professional and personal lives, and may you find your work deeply rewarding.

The Aga Khan University is now twenty years old, but its aspirations were formed in the 1970s, nearly a generation ago. Some ten years ago, the Chancellor's Commission reexamined the University's goals and intentions as set down in the Harvard Report of 1983 and found them to be no less salient. The commission strongly reaffirmed AKU's commitment to be, in its words, an "open, Muslim university, devoted to free inquiry of distinction, quality and international character, preparing its students for constructive, worthwhile and responsible roles in society."

There were questions in AKU's early years about the timeliness and priority of a university in an environment in which poverty and illiteracy—as we knew only too well—were dauntingly high. Would a new university and its university hospital merely benefit well-prepared students and well-off patients, replicating existing social divisions? It is only in the last few years that new voices, such as the World Bank's, have noted the world's "knowledge revolution," in which it is not so much factories, land and machinery that drive the world economy but the knowledge, skills and resourcefulness of people. All societies, it has become clear, must invest in higher education for their talented men and women or risk being relegated to subordinate, vulnerable positions in the world.

The feelings of the subordination of people—that they are victims of an economic or cultural globalization in which they cannot be full partners but from which they cannot remain apart—these feelings fuel some of the most potent, destructive forces at play in our world today. The sense of vulnerability is especially powerful in parts of the Muslim world, which is heir to one of the greatest civilizations the world has known but which also has inherited from history not of its making some of the worst and longest conflicts of the last one hundred years, those of the Middle East and Kashmir. When people of a distinctive faith or culture feel economically powerless, or inherit clear injustice from which they cannot escape, or find their traditions and values engulfed culturally and their societies maligned as bleak and unjust, some among them can too readily become vulnerable. They risk becoming the victims of those who would gain power by perverting an open, fluid, pluralistic tradition of thought and belief into something closed and insular.

It would be wrong to see this possibility as the future of the Ummah. Many today across the Muslim world know their history and deeply value their heritage but are also keenly sensitive to the radically altered conditions of the modern world. They realize, too, how erroneous and unreasonable it is to believe that there is an unbridgeable divide between their heritage and the modern world. There is clearly a need to mitigate what is not a "clash of civilizations" but a "clash of ignorance," in which peoples of different faiths or cultural traditions are so ignorant of each other that they are unable to find a common language with which to communicate. Those with an educated and enlightened approach—among whom I count our graduates—are of the firm, sincere conviction that their societies can benefit from modernity while remaining true to tradition. They will be the bridge that can eliminate forever today's dangerous clash of ignorance.

It is especially at times when ignorance, conflict and apprehension are so rife that universities, both in the Muslim world and in the West, have a greater obligation to promote intellectual openness and tolerance and to create increased cultural understanding. Muslim universities, however, have a unique responsibility: to engender in their societies a new confidence. It must be a confidence based on intellectual excellence but also on a refreshed, enlightened appreciation of the scientific, linguistic, artistic and religious traditions that underpin and give such global value to our own Muslim civilizations, even though these traditions may be ignored or not understood by parts of the Ummah itself. In the twenty years since the granting of its charter, the AKU has made a good beginning.

The School of Nursing in Pakistan and eastern Africa have become known internationally for the professional competence of their graduates and the value to Asia and Africa of their curricula and pedagogy. I am delighted that today we award the University's first postgraduate diplomas to two graduates of the Master's program in Nursing. This is the first time in Pakistan that postgraduate degrees in Nursing have been offered, and I view it as a major achievement not only for the nursing profession but for higher education for women in Pakistan and the Muslim world.

Graduates of the Medical College have established the reputation of their scientific and clinical preparation through residencies in excellent teaching hospitals around the world. Medical College faculty members have proven themselves to be talented instructors and clinicians of the highest standards in their respective specializations at the University Hospital. The hospital itself is now certified to meet stringent international standards of care. It continues to respond swiftly to major emergencies in Karachi. And I am especially pleased that its outreach services in Pakistan, in such areas as family medicine, home physiotherapy and laboratory tests, will by the end of the year have treated some two million patients.

The Institute for Educational Development, helped greatly by grants from the international community, is revitalizing teaching and curricular improvement in schools in Pakistan, Central Asia, the Middle East and eastern Africa. The institute is working hard to develop research-based educational policy making.

I do not minimize these achievements, nor do I ignore the importance of the University's continuing investment in its buildings, laboratories, instrumentation and precious faculty resources, when I say that AKU now has the strength and the duty to tackle an array of new challenges. AKU's earliest planners foresaw most of these challenges, but the perils and voids of understanding I have suggested give them particular urgency now.

First, the university must continue to expand its programs of research. The true sign of maturity and excellence in a university is its ability to contribute to the knowledge of humankind, in its own society and beyond. It is equally essential that its faculty be challenged, as a matter of university policy, to expand the boundaries of human knowledge. Any vestige of dependence is cast off, any suspicion by a young scientist or scholar that he or she may sacrifice intellectual excitement by leaving the West is allayed, when a university becomes known for generating new ideas, making new discoveries and influencing events.

Some of this research will be in advanced realms of the medical sciences. AKU and Pakistan must be part of the international edifice of inquiry in fields such as microbiology and biochemistry that will contribute to the quality of human life in the coming century. Because this is AKU, such work will usually be targeted in an area, such as hypertension, of great concern to the people of Pakistan.

Much AKU research, however, will focus on pressing issues of public policy. This naturally follows the precepts of Islam that applying scientific reason, building society and refining human aspirations and ethics should always reinforce one another. The University, most notably the Department of Community Health Sciences, is already developing strength in applied research. This growth has enabled it to develop very productive relations among AKU scholars and scientists and provincial, federal and aid agency policy makers in such fields as nutrition, educational testing, maternal and child health, immunization strategies, vaccine development and epidemiology.

So important are this growing research capacity and informed discourse with policy makers that the University must strengthen its public policy commitment. Large problem areas, from human development and bioethics to economic growth and human settlements, desperately need systematic thought and information. Whether through an

Institute of Public Policy, policy units in existing departments or even fully developed new faculties, AKU will pledge its energies and imagination to advancing effective public policy.

The second new emphasis of AKU will gradually and beneficially change the university's nature: *internationalization*. By the terms of its charter, AKU is to be an international university, with programs, projects, institutes and campuses in other countries that have the desire, capacity and collegial spirit for partnership. The times I have described make these partnerships especially valuable today, and over time they will broaden and greatly strengthen the university.

AKU has made a good beginning in East Africa. In collaboration with Aga Khan Hospitals and Health Services, the School of Nursing has established Advanced Nursing Programs in Kenya, Uganda and Tanzania with the encouragement of those governments. This is the first time in the history of medical education in eastern Africa that a private-sector network of institutions is offering medical degrees. Postgraduate medical education for physicians, assisted by our Medical College, will soon follow in these countries. In the field of education, AKU will soon establish in East Africa a new Institute for Educational Development, with its model, tested for a decade in Pakistan, of Professional Development Centres for teacher improvement and curriculum development. These centres will work both with national schools and with the first Aga Khan Schools of Excellence, private boarding schools of international quality now being established in East Africa. The objective of these schools is to enable means-blind, merit-based access to educational and extracurricular facilities of the highest international standards with multilingual curricula based on the International Baccalaureate program. There will, *inshallah*, eventually be up to twenty-one such Schools of Excellence in numerous countries in Africa, Central Asia and South Asia. Students and faculty will be encouraged to live and learn from all that this multinational network of schools can offer, circulating extensively within it. New generations of teachers and graduates with multilingual competencies and a new understanding of human pluralism should emerge. Some of these men and women will return to educate students at AKU's Institute for Educational Development here in Pakistan and the future one to be created in East Africa. Others will teach at the Professional Development Centres. Hopefully this will result in a significant enhancement of the professional standing and strength of teachers in Asia and Africa. In due course, it is possible to imagine a full, comprehensive AKU campus in East Africa with strengths in educational development, health sciences education and public policy.

The University is also working now in Afghanistan, where the School of Nursing is helping to increase the capacities of the six Intermediate Medical Education Institutes; in Syria, where we see the beginnings of productive work with the Ministry of Education; and in Central Asia, with the University of Central Asia recently established by an international treaty between the Ismaili Imamat and the governments of Tajikistan, Kyrgyzstan and Kazakhstan.

I strongly believe as these international associations increase, it will become clear that although AKU's immediate goal is to provide assistance, its long-term goal is not the mere extension of its existing skills but the enhancement of its core purposes with partners of equal strength in different cultural settings. When this happens, AKU will be a most exciting innovation: a genuinely international, intercultural university, exchanging students and faculty among campuses that share a common goal of intellectual excellence.

My third aspiration is that AKU now fulfill its mission to become a comprehensive university and a centre of liberal study of Muslim civilizations. Muslim scholars in South and Central Asia, the Middle East and sub-Saharan Africa are researching, publishing and discussing far too few books on Muslim history, architecture, city planning, art, philosophy, economics, and languages and literatures. There is too little public sustenance for, and debate about, contemporary Muslim architecture and literature—and relatively little of the literary, cinematic and musical talent from Turkey, Egypt and Iran that is now beginning to be recognized. The consequences are an intelligentsia—and a younger, successor generation—that is intellectually unchallenged and culturally undernourished, and a one-way flow of scholarship and popular culture from the West, which, in turn, receives all too little that is creative, interpretative, scholarly and artistic from the Muslim world.

In the coming decade, I believe AKU can help, less to fill a void than to become a magnet and a concentration for Muslim scholars who are vividly engaged in a broad range of humanistic studies. AKU's Institute of the Study of

Muslim Civilizations in London is making a beginning. It is assembling scholars from around the Arabic-, Farsi- and Urdu-speaking parts of the Muslim world in the fields of philosophy, history and other disciplines. Through public seminars and research monographs on a variety of topics— ethics, ecology, historiography, scholarly traditions and dimensions of Muslim identity—they will develop and test the curriculum of an MA in Muslim Civilizations that will be of value to the liberal professions, including diplomats, teachers, businesspeople, publishers, journalists, civil servants and NGO professionals.

The hub of this scholarly venture will be the AKU's new Faculty of Arts and Sciences, which will be well underway in the present decade. The Faculty will establish a residential campus on 600 acres of land that the University has purchased to the northeast of Karachi. In its first phase, it will have 1,400 to 1,500 undergraduates and some 100 postgraduate students. Undergraduates will experience rigorous pedagogy in English and receive education in the sciences, economics and information technology. But they will also, with equal rigour, be expected to master a broad core curriculum that engages them in world history, in the study of one or more Asian languages, and in strong foundation courses on the elements of Muslim civilizations, on South Asian history and culture, and on the history of the Persian-speaking world. They will also perform summer service and research projects in rural and urban areas of their own societies.

Such interdisciplinary programs as Human Development, Government, Law and Public Policy, Human Settlements and Architecture will function at both undergraduate and postgraduate levels and will prefigure eventual professional schools. Graduates of these programs will be qualified for further study, or employment, anywhere in the world. The objective of the new undergraduate faculty is to equip young men and women from within and outside the Ummah with the skills, ethical commitment and leadership qualities for their future careers, wherever they choose to lead them. My great hope and prayer is that, in time to come, the Aga Khan University will be only one of hundreds of universities in the Muslim world that are on the frontiers of scientific and humanistic knowledge, radiating intelligence and confidence, research and graduates, into flourishing economies and progressive legal and political systems.

I hold these aspirations for the Aga Khan University, but I also hold them for our new graduates. I hope that both AKU and you, our 2003 graduates, continue to be restless researchers and learners. I hope that you, like AKU, will, with broadened international and cultural horizons, recall the heritage of Muslim civilizations past and discover that change and progress take time but that they also require impatience.

CANADA AS A GLOBAL LEADER

GOVERNOR GENERAL'S
LEADERSHIP CONFERENCE

Gatineau, Canada, May 19, 2004

IT IS A JOY and a privilege to address the young leaders of
Canada, who represent different walks of national life
as well as Canada's social, cultural and regional diversity. I
am particularly happy at this opportunity, as you have been
jointly exploring a critical aspect of the role of leadership:
how leadership—political and civil—can help sustain the
moral and dynamic coherence in public life that Canada
has so successfully constructed, predicated on the ethic of
respect for human dignity. This coherence recognizes and
builds on difference, enables a spirit of compromise and
consensus in public and legislative policies, and marks out a
healthy space for the role of civil society as a sound—indeed
an essential—bulwark for democratic processes.

Canada has an experience of governance of which much
of the world stands in dire need. It is a world of increasing

dissension and conflict, in which different ethnic, tribal, religious or social groups have often failed to search for, and agree upon, a common space for harmonious coexistence. This situation of conflict and instability poses a grave risk for the future relationship between the industrialized world and the developing world. The polarizing and paralyzing Cold War, which impacted millions of people in the developing world, has gone. The new issue that demands the attention of the international community is the need to create stable states with self-sustainable economies and stable, inclusive forms of governance.

Much of the world's attention is periodically focussed on the phenomenon of so-called failed states. But of the global threats that face us today, apart from nuclear war or HIV/AIDS, the most preoccupying is not failed states. It is the failure of democracy. The global picture at the beginning of the twenty-first century is a story of failed democracies in the Muslim world, in Latin America, in eastern Europe and in sub-Saharan Africa. A startling fact today is that nearly 40 per cent of UN member nations are failed democracies. The greatest risk to the West itself, and to its values, is therefore the accumulation of failed democracies, which, in turn, will cause deep undercurrents of stress, if not conflict, among societies. It is essential, in its own interest, that the West admit to itself that democracy is as fragile as any other form of human governance.

It is essential that every nation and each society ask the following question: "If democracy is failing, why is this the case?" They must make every effort to help correct the situation rather than referring dismissively to "failed states." To my knowledge, democracy can fail anywhere, at any time, in any society—as it has in several well-known and well-documented situations in Europe, as recently as the last fifty years. It is self-evident, in Europe and across the globe, that the existence of political parties and elections does not alone produce stable governments or competent leadership.

Three concepts seem to me essential in creating, stabilizing and strengthening democracy around the world, including among the people of Africa and Asia with whom I have worked in the past. These concepts are meritocracy, pluralism and civil society. What role can Canada play, drawing upon its national genius, in creating or enhancing these great underpinnings of democracy in the developing world?

A recent UN audit of democracy, covering eighteen Latin American countries, reemphasizes the virtues of democracy in advancing human development. But it also warns that stagnant per capita incomes and growing inequality, in access to civil rights as well as in income, are producing doubt, impatience and civil unrest. Thus, the report underlines a key concept that you will all know instinctively and that my experience working in the developing world has illustrated decade after decade: the primary daily concern of peoples everywhere is their quality of life, which is intimately connected to their value systems. The report recognizes a crucial fact: "An important relationship exists between citizenship and organizations of civil society, which are major actors in the strengthening of democracy, in the oversight of government stewardship and in the development of pluralism."

My interest in these themes of development and governance arises from my role as the hereditary spiritual leader—Imam—of the Shia Ismaili Muslim community. Culturally very diverse, the Ismailis are spread across the globe, mostly as a minority, in more than twenty-five countries in South and Central Asia, the Middle East and sub-Saharan Africa. In recent decades they have also established a substantial presence in Canada, the U.S.A. and western Europe. Since succeeding to this office as the forty-ninth Imam in 1957, I have been concerned with the development of the Ismailis and the broader societies in which they live. The engagement of the Imamat in development is guided by Islamic ethics, which bridge faith and society. It is on this premise that I established the Aga Khan Development Network. This network of agencies has long been active in many areas of Asia and Africa to improve the quality of life of all who live there. These areas are home to some of the poorest and most diverse populations in the world. Our long presence on the ground gives us an insight that confirms the UN's detailed assessment in Latin America, which is that a democracy cannot function reasonably without two preconditions.

The first is a healthy civil society. It is an essential bulwark that provides citizens with multiple channels through which to exercise effectively both their rights and their duties of citizenship. Even at a very basic level, only a strong civil society can ensure both isolated rural populations and the marginalized urban poor a reasonable prospect of humane treatment, personal security, equity, the absence of discrimination and access to opportunity.

The second precondition is pluralism. Pluralism means peoples of diverse backgrounds and interests coming together in organizations of varying types and goals, for different forms of creative expression, which are valuable and deserving of support by government and society as a whole.

The rejection of pluralism is pervasive across the globe, and this rejection plays a significant role in breeding destructive conflicts. Examples are scattered across the world's map: in Asia, in the Middle East, in Africa, in Europe, in the Americas. No continent has been spared the tragedies of death, of misery or of the persecution of minorities. Are such high-risk situations predictable? If the answer is yes, then what can be done about them, to pre-empt the risk that the rejection of pluralism will become the spark that sets human conflict aflame? Is the onus not on leadership, in all parts of the world, to build a knowledge base about such situations and consider strategies for preventing them? I deeply believe our collective conscience must accept that pluralism is no less important than human rights for ensuring peace, successful democracy and a better quality of life.

I am optimistic that much constructive work can be done, and I would cite one example—from the forty years of experience of the Aga Khan Development Network's agencies—in which the careful, patient development of civil society institutions helped to create the capacity to manage and legitimize pluralism. In Northern Pakistan, once one of the poorest areas on earth, our Network has been working for over twenty years, with CIDA, the Canadian International Development Agency, as our lead partner. Isolated and bypassed rural communities of different ethnic and religious backgrounds—Shia, Sunni and non-Muslim—struggled to eke out a meagre living, farming small holdings in the harsh environment of this mountain desert ecosystem. Relations among the communities were often hostile. The challenge for the Network was to create sustainable, inclusive processes of development in which diverse communities could participate and seek joint solutions to common problems.

To summarize two decades of our work there: over 3,900 village-based organizations, comprising a mix of broad-based representations and interest-specific groups in such fields as women's initiatives, water usage, and savings and credit were established. The quality of life for 1.3 million people living in a rural environment, representative of the majority of the population of Asia and Africa, has dramatically improved. Per capita income has increased by 300 per cent, savings have soared, and male and female education, primary health, housing, sanitation and cultural awareness have seen major improvements. Former antagonists have debated and worked together to create new programs and social structures in Northern Pakistan, and, more recently, in Tajikistan. Consensus about hope for the future has replaced conflict born of despair and memories of the past.

This micro-experiment with grassroots democracy, civil society and pluralism has also underlined, for everyone involved, the enormous importance of competence and advancement by merit. Inherent in the notion of merit is the idea of equality of access to opportunities. Citizens who possess potential, whatever the community to which they belong, can realize their potential only if they have access to good education, good health and prospects to advance through enterprise. Without this equity, merit does not develop.

A secure pluralistic society requires communities that are educated and confident in the identity and depth of both their own traditions and those of their neighbours. Democracies must be educated if they are to express themselves competently and their electorates are to reach informed opinions about the great issues at stake. Perhaps the greatest obstacle to pluralism and democracy, however, is the lacuna in the general education of the populations involved. A dramatic illustration is the uninformed speculation about conflict between the Muslim world and others. The clash, if there is such a broad civilizational collision, is not of cultures but of ignorance. How many leaders, even in the West, whether in politics, the media or other professions that shape public opinion, grow up aware that the historical root cause of the conflict in the Middle East was an outcome of the First World War? Or that the tragedy that is Kashmir is an unresolved colonial legacy? Or that neither situation had anything to do with the faith of Islam? To what extent is the public aware that the deployment of Afghanistan as a proxy by both sides in the Cold War is a major factor in that country's recent history of tragic woes? These matters, which now touch the lives of all world citizens, are simply not addressed at any level of general education in most Western countries.

Humanities curricula in Western educational institutions rarely feature the great Muslim philosophers, scientists, astronomers and writers of the classical age of Islam, such as Avicenna, al-Farabi and al-Kindi, Nasir Khusraw and Tusi. This lack of knowledge and appreciation of the civilizations of the Muslim world colours media stereotypes, causing the media to concentrate on political hot spots in the Muslim world and refer to organizations as terrorist and Islamic first, and then only obliquely, if at all, to their national origins or political goals.

No wonder the bogey of Islam as a monolith, irreconcilable to the values of the West, or worse, as a seedbed of violence, lurks behind the depiction of Islam as being both opposed to and incapable of pluralism. This image flies directly in the face of the respect Islam's cherished scripture confers upon believers in monotheistic traditions, calling upon Muslims to engage with them in the finest manner, and with wisdom. History is replete with illustrations of Muslims entrusting their most treasured possessions, even members of their families, to the care of Christians. Muslim willingness to learn from Jewish erudition in medicine, statecraft and other realms of knowledge is well exemplified by the place of honour accorded Jewish scholars at the court of the Fatimid Imam-Caliphs of Egypt.

Intellectual honesty and greater knowledge are essential if current explosive situations are to be understood as inherited conflicts and—rather than being specific to the Muslim world—driven by ethnic and demographic difference, economic inequity and unresolved political situations.

An excellent example of what is needed to shape national sentiments, as well as to guide foreign policy in this perilous time, is the recent parliamentary committee report entitled "Exploring Canada's Relations with the Countries of the Muslim World." I wish there were time to comment on a number of the observations in the report, but in its very opening sentence, which begins, "The dynamic complexity and diversity of the Muslim world," the report sets the tone of balance and wisdom that suffuse its recommendations. It emphasizes history, education and the urgent need for communication and general knowledge in observing, "Understanding Islamic influences on government and state policies, on social and economic relations, cultural norms, individual and group rights and the like, necessarily goes far beyond the question of the extreme, violent-minority edges of Islamist activity." I warmly hope that the resources can be found to bring to life the constructive recommendations of this fine report, as the need for such rational voices is great. It is urgent that the West gain a better understanding of the Islamic world, which, as the report notes, is a hugely diverse collectivity of civilizations that has developed, and continues to evolve, in response to multiple societal influences—agricultural and rural, commercial and urban, scientific and philosophical, literary and political. Just like other great traditions, the Islamic world cannot be understood only by its faith, but as a total picture whose history is closely tied to that of the Judeo-Christian world.

In this situation of a conflict of ignorance between the Muslim world and the West, an example of Canada's bridging is the support given by CIDA and McMaster University to the Aga Khan University School of Nursing. Not only did this partnership transform nursing education and the nursing profession in Pakistan, but it is now having a significant impact in Kenya, Tanzania, Uganda, Afghanistan and Syria, by offering women in these countries new and respected professional opportunities.

Canada is in an almost unique position to broaden the scope of its engagement with the developing world by sharing very widely its experience in humane governance to support pluralism, the development of civil society and meritocratic premises for action. For instance, incipient, homegrown civil society institutions in developing countries need expert assistance to strengthen their capacities for management, program design and implementation, fundraising, self-study and evaluation. They require help in such other areas as defining answerability and the criteria that measure success, as well as in identifying how a sector can be financed and sustained. I am happy to note that this is the declared intention of your government. In the words of Prime Minister Paul Martin, speaking in the House of Commons: "One of the distinct ways in which Canada can help developing nations is to provide the expertise and experience of Canadians in justice, in federalism, in pluralist democracy."

In living through its history and confronting its challenges, Canada has established strong institutions to sustain democracy, the cornerstone of which is your multifaceted, robust civil society. Canada offers the world an example of meshing, and thereby fortifying, civil society with merit from all segments of its population. You are, hence, able to harness the best from different groups, because your civil society is not bound by a specific language or race or religion.

My intention is not to embarrass you with too rosy a picture of the Canadian mosaic, as if it were free of all tension. But you have the experience, an infrastructure grounded in wisdom and the moral wherewithal to be able to handle challenges to your social and political fabric.

The Ismaili Imamat strives to ensure that people live in countries where the threat to democracy is minimal and seeks to draw on the experience of established democracies that have a vibrant civil society, are sensitive to cultural difference and are effective in improving the quality of life of their citizenry. Canada is a prime example of such a country. It is for this reason that the Aga Khan Development Network is establishing, in Ottawa, what is to be known as the Global Centre for Pluralism.

This secular, non-denominational centre will engage in education and research and will also examine the experience of pluralism in practice. Drawing on Canadian expertise, and working closely with governments, academia and civil society, the Centre will seek to foster enabling legislative and policy environments. Its particular emphasis will be on strengthening indigenous capacity for research and policy analysis on pluralism while also offering educational, professional development and public awareness programs.

Ladies and gentlemen: There are compelling reasons, as I have tried to articulate, why Canada can and should take the lead in investing to safeguard and enhance pluralism. We inhabit an overcrowded planet with shrinking resources, yet we share a common destiny. A weakness or pain in one corner has the tendency, rather rapidly, to transmit itself across the globe. Instability is infectious. But so is hope. It is for you—the leaders of today and tomorrow—to carry the torch of that hope and help to share the gift of pluralism.

REFERENCES .

Canada. "Exploring Canada's Relations with the Countries of the Muslim World." Committee Chair: Bernard Patry. (Ottawa: Standing Committee on Foreign Affairs and International Trade, 2004). http://cmte.parl.gc.ca/Content/HOC/committee/373/fait/reports/rp1281987/faitrp01/faitrp01-e.pdf.

Martin, Paul. Address by the prime minister in reply to the Speech from the Throne to open the third session of the thirty-seventh Parliament of Canada. February 3, 2004.

United Nations Development Programme (UNDP). *Democracy in Latin America: Towards a Citizens' Democracy* (New York: United Nations Development Programme, 2004). www.undp.org/democracy_report_latin_america/Ideas_and_Contributions.pdf.

THE NATURE OF TRUE REGIME CHANGE

ONTARIO INSTITUTE *for* STUDIES *in*
EDUCATION, UNIVERSITY *of* TORONTO, UPON
RECEIVING *an* HONORARY DOCTORATE

Toronto, Canada, June 18, 2004

I AM DEEPLY MOVED by the honour that this renowned institution of learning has done of conferring upon me the degree of Doctor of Laws, *honoris causa*. I accept this award with much happiness but also a profound sense of humility, cognizant that many men and women of higher distinction and more notable achievements are also being recognized, joining an illustrious line of previous recipients.

But above all, today's event belongs to you, the graduands of the Ontario Institute for Studies in Education, as you contemplate the nature of the world that awaits your engagement. From your choice of education as the area of knowledge of greatest interest to you, there are at least three questions I assume you will apply to most of your future endeavours. First, what will future generations of educated people in Canada and around the world need to know to earn honourable livelihoods for themselves and their families? Second, what will future generations need to know to make our world a better place? And third, what can you, as Canadians, do to play an optimized world role?

In 1957, the year I became Imam of the Shia Ismaili Muslims, the Nobel Peace Prize winner was a sixty-year-old statesman who, two years earlier, in a book entitled *Democracy in World Politics,* had written: "We are now emerging into an age when different civilizations will have to learn to live side by side in peaceful interchange, learning from each other, studying each other's history and ideals, art and culture, mutually enriching each other's lives. The only alternative, in this overcrowded little world, is misunderstanding, tension, clash, and catastrophe." The prescient writer, whom some of you will recognize as a distinguished alumnus and former teacher at this great institution, went on to lead this country as its fourteenth prime minister: Lester B. Pearson.

Four weeks ago, speaking at the Leadership and Diversity Conference in Ottawa, I noted that some 40 per cent of the countries in the United Nations are failed democracies, and the UN's own experience points to the general weak state of civil society in these countries as one of the major causes for this widespread failure. What is civil society? Why is it so essential to the good health of any modern state? And what is the role of education in shaping and enriching civil society?

The World Bank uses the term to refer to a wide array of organizations that have a presence in public life but are not affiliated with the state. They function on a not-for-profit basis to express the interests and values of their members and others, based on ethical, cultural, political, scientific, religious or philanthropic considerations. In this sense, civil society organizations are multifarious: from community and indigenous groups through faith-based and charitable organizations, to non-governmental organizations (NGOs), labour unions, professional associations and foundations. But a broader definition holds that civil society embraces an even wider diversity of spaces, actors and institutional forms that vary in their degree of formality, autonomy and power. Besides the World Bank's categories, these spaces are populated by such organizations as village and women's groups, neighbourhood self-help groups, social movements, business associations, microcredit organizations, coalitions and advocacy groups.

In an era of rising expectations and unmet needs in the developed and—much more—in the developing world, civil society institutions play an essential role in providing social services, protecting the marginalized and delivering development programs. The positive action of these civil society initiatives is especially critical where governments are weak or non-performing, as in situations of failed democracies or post-conflict reconciliation and reconstruction.

Whatever definition is used, a quality civil society is independent of government; it is pluralist, and it is led by merit-based, educated leadership. Not only does Canadian civil society eminently meet these three criteria, but I know of no country where civil society is more empathetic with the needs of civil society in the countries of Africa and Asia, countries in which I have been working for some forty-five years. I have therefore asked myself, not once but hundreds of times, if and how Canadian civil society can mobilize its resources more vigorously to help improve the quality of life of the peoples of Africa and Asia.

Asked in these terms, the issue becomes that of sharing the many forms of human knowledge and experience that create and sustain a civil society of quality, rather than looking for a massive injection of monetary resources. There are, however, two obvious preconditions. First, that the governments and peoples of the developing world wish for, and welcome, the help being offered. This requires an enabling social, legal and fiscal environment. Second, that Canadian institutions and human resources must see real enrichment in life's purpose in their willingness to help.

Assuming these preconditions are met, you may ask how this wide civil society partnership for development can occur in practice. Innumerable forms have achieved genuine successes in the past. These include the sharing of best practices; the twinning of institutions; quality improvement in the delivery of health care and education; secondment of leadership such as school head teachers or university professors in specialized fields; the strengthening of civil society institutions in forward programming and performance measurement; the continuing education of those in the most marginalized professions, such as nursing or journalism; and the teaching of best practices in the not-for-profit and charity fields. The opportunities for partnership are many.

But they are not being realized—or if they are, they are occurring at a level infinitely below the needs and dramatically below the potential for change. This is the nature of the true regime change we need, where the civil society of the industrialized world gives wide, encompassing support to that of the developing world. True regime change occurs when liberty is guaranteed by a people free to create or support institutions of their own choosing. True regime change occurs when that strength and that freedom are defined by the depth, breadth and quality of education shared across the society in question.

Partnerships between the developed and developing worlds can and do work. Moreover, they demonstrate how essential universities and their lifeblood—you, their graduates—are to civil society. Today, in Pakistan, the Kyrgyz Republic and Tanzania, at the forefront of curricular change and new teaching technologies, are young men and women who, like yourselves, have studied at OISE. They are graduates of the Aga Khan University's Institute for Educational Development, which was established with the help of the universities of Toronto and Oxford. Today, also, the Aga Khan University is collaborating with international research institutions in the developed world in areas ranging from cancer and HIV/AIDS to cardiovascular disease, perinatal infection and hypertension. These collaborations, across national, cultural, linguistic, religious and ethnic boundaries, are serving to find ways of preserving life. At the nascent University of Central Asia, we are researching and addressing the challenges of mountain societies, drawing on a multiplicity of traditions to create stability and prosperity in remote yet geopolitically sensitive regions of the world—preserving not just life but societies, cultures and perhaps nations.

Today, you are graduating from one of Canada's greatest universities in a field of study that is of paramount importance. I am speaking to you as a person whose roots and institutional engagement are in the developing world; as a Muslim; as someone seeking to engage with and improve the lives of the millions of people who live in Asia and Africa. It is against this background that I invite you—indeed, I urge you—to reflect deeply on the needs of our world today. I am sure you will wish to seize the opportunities for sharing your knowledge with future generations here in Canada, but should you wish it, the reach of your knowledge can go far beyond your shores and will be deeply welcomed. Because civil society is so critical to the quality of life and the pace of progress, and because it finds expression in so many pluralist forms and spaces, I am convinced that the future before you, in this global environment we share, offers you a remarkable spectrum of opportunities.

REFERENCE

Pearson, Lester B. *Democracy in World Politics*. Princeton: Princeton University Press, 1955.

UNDERWRITING HUMAN PROGRESS

I WILL TALK TO you today about an issue that has been a critical focus for most of my working life: the process of social, cultural and economic development in many of the poorest regions of the world. In particular, I will attempt to go some way towards answering this fundamental question: what are the preconditions for developing countries to be transformed into peaceful and productive modern societies?

As I look at escalating tensions in the world I am convinced more than ever that neither peaceful nor productive modern societies will ever be achieved by short-term responses composed in the midst of crisis. What I will propose to you today is that there are fundamental issues that must be addressed persistently, and over the long term, if we are to achieve the desired outcomes.

My views are presented from two perspectives. First, as the hereditary spiritual leader—Imam—of the Shia Ismaili Muslim community. Like the Muslim Ummah as a whole, the Ismailis are culturally diverse. They are settled across the globe as minorities in more than twenty-five countries. There are Ismaili communities in South and Central Asia, the Middle East and sub-Saharan Africa. In recent decades Ismailis have also established a substantial presence in western Europe and North America through migration.

The second perspective is that of someone who has been engaged in human and economic development in many of the most fragile regions of the world for more than forty-five years, and whose roots and institutional commitments are there.

The engagement of the Imamat in development is guided by the ethics of Islam that bridge faith and society, a premise on which I established the Aga Khan Development Network, known as the AKDN. Its cultural, social and economic development agencies seek to improve opportunities and living conditions of the weakest in society, without regard to their origin, gender or faith. We work with many partners, including scores of national and international agencies. Several of my observations today apply to developing countries generally. But our greatest depth of experience is in countries with substantial or majority Muslim populations. Therefore, my comments will make particular reference to matters as they affect the Muslim world, including Africa, Asia and the Near and Middle East.

I will begin by quoting from Minister Fischer's remarks to the fortieth Munich Conference on Security Policy this past February. He noted that efforts to foster peace and security must go far beyond security matters alone. He said, and I quote: "Social and cultural modernization issues, as well as democracy, the rule of law, women's rights and good governance, are of almost even greater importance."

Minister Fischer was referring specifically to dealing with the issue of terrorism. I certainly agree with his point about that. I also believe the issues he raises are of broad and permanent concern to the developing world. Even in parts of the developing world where terrorism is not an issue, improving the quality of life is critically dependent upon advances in the areas he identified.

I would like to focus today on what I believe are three essential pre-conditions for the successful transition of the poorest areas of the world into modern, peaceful societies. They are stable and competent democratic governance; an environment that respects and encourages pluralism, and a diverse and engaged civil society. In my view, these must be critical components of any global development policy. Not only are they mutually reinforcing, they also permit developing societies to gradually become masters of the process and to make that process ultimately sustainable.

I believe we must work in each of these areas simultaneously. But we should not expect to make progress in each one at an equal pace. Nor should we plan for them to occur in sequence. We must also anticipate and plan for setbacks and failures. This requires a multilateral deployment of resources for capacity building. Otherwise, millions suffer while we await perfection.

Let us look first at democracy. In the 1990s, the term "failed state" gained currency to describe the situation in places like Afghanistan and Bosnia or Liberia and Somalia. Today, such descriptions simply divert attention from the real issues. Apart from weapons of mass destruction, HIV/ AIDS and climate change, the greatest global threat today is not failed states—states themselves do not fail—but the failure of democracy in nearly 40 per cent of UN member nations. These failures cross much of the Muslim world, Latin America, eastern Europe and Africa.

In my visits to African countries such as Mali and Uganda, to Middle East countries such as Syria, and to Asian countries such as Kyrgyzstan and Pakistan, leaders in all levels of society have expressed to me their deep concern and frustration about the failure of democracy and its consequent inability to put governments in authority that can meet the expectations of the people. They would welcome assistance in supporting education about democracy. Unfortunately today, in more and more developing countries where there is a tradition of legislative elections, we are witnessing a splintering of national political parties into factions based around narrow interests. Coalition governments are being cobbled together by leaders with little experience in managing multiple factions.

We need only look at the recent history of western Europe to understand the difficulty such coalition governments may face in delivering effective, democratic governance. For many years, the lifespan of governments in some countries was measured in months. Building consensus for corrective constitutional changes, and implementing those changes, was equally challenging. What logic is there to think, therefore, that an African government suddenly having to manage a fractious coalition after years of single-party majorities will be able to address this issue maturely? If it cannot, how will it meet the expectations of its people for a better life?

The point is this: democracy is fragile. It is susceptible to failure at any time, in any society. The experience of Europe in the last fifty years should also be a sobering reminder of another unfortunate truism. Elections and the existence of political parties do not by themselves guarantee stable governments, competent political leadership and respect for the constitution. Nor do they guarantee good economic management and the absence of corruption. If this has been the experience in the birthplace of modern democracy, I must urge you to be patiently supportive of democratic experiments in the Middle East and in the wider developing world.

Sometimes I read that Islam is in conflict with democracy. Yet I must tell you that, as a Muslim, I am a democrat not because of Greek or French thought but primarily because of principles that go back 1,400 years, directly after the death of Prophet Muhammad (peace be upon him).

At that time, Muslims debated how best to implement the premises he had established for being qualified for leadership. The principle of wide public consultation in selecting leadership for matters relating to affairs of state and civil administration was adopted by groups that coalesced into the Sunni branch. The parallel principle of hereditary leadership was preserved among the Shia. Muslims of the time also established that leadership in social governance was to be selected on the basis of merit and competence. These principles, cemented fourteen centuries ago, are consistent with democratic models that exist around the world today.

A quick analysis of the map of the Near and Middle East shows the strong probability that numerous forms of democratic government will be tested in the coming decades. Some states will test republican democracy, others will test constitutional monarchy, and yet others will test various forms of theocratic government. It is impossible to predict the outcomes or the pace of change. What we can predict with some certainty is that the kaleidoscope of changing patterns will be driven by internal forces, as has already been illustrated in Iraq and Afghanistan. Personally, I do not see how it could be otherwise, given the multiplicity of stakeholders and the absolute necessity that all must be consulted if consensus is to be achieved and maintained. Therefore, I strongly believe these indigenous elements must be nurtured and supported. We must ensure that they have a solid grasp of the elements that sustain, or weaken, democracy and its institutions.

Any development strategy, therefore, must include education and support for developing a wider understanding of the institutions and processes of constitutional democracy. Formal education, beginning at the secondary school level, can play a part. But so too can such programs as exchanges of working groups of parliamentarians, legislative officers, senior government officials, and the panoply of civil society participants, including journalists, educators and lawyers. We must seek to build breadth and depth of understanding of the culture of democracy, both in theory and in application.

Let me turn now to the issue of pluralism. We have all witnessed how inattention to, or worse, the rejection of, pluralism has bred destructive conflicts across the globe affecting a great many cultures, races, nationalities and religions. Sadly, these insights have been dramatically reinforced by events in such varied situations as Afghanistan, Tajikistan, Rwanda and the Democratic Republic of Congo. These events underline how fundamental it is in the developing world for democracy to be built around an absolute priority to manage and legitimize pluralism.

Pluralist societies do not happen by themselves, as accidents of history. They are a product of enlightened education and continuous investment by government and all forces of civil society in developing value and recognition for one of humanity's greatest assets: the diversity of its peoples. Is it not therefore the responsibility of enlightened leadership everywhere to ensure that pluralism, and education about pluralism, occupy centre stage in any agenda of global priorities?

And yet school curricula in Western and developing countries rarely give young people a sound understanding of their own cultures, let alone the diverse religious, linguistic, social and artistic forces of communities around them. These perceptions have led the AKDN's primary and

secondary schools, and particularly its new network of academic centres of excellence, the Aga Khan Academies, to
experiment with education curricula that make the case for
a pluralist worldview. It is one that builds on differences of
outlook, ethnicity, religion and culture. This initiative will
benefit from collaboration with some of the leading international schools, including Salem in Germany, that are
working with us in an international academic partnership.

It is my profound belief that the Judeo-Christian world
will find it a hopeless endeavour to try to address the issues
of democracy, civil society and pluralism in the Muslim
world unless a major effort—and I mean an absolutely major
effort—is made by Judeo-Christians to acquire deeper and
wider knowledge about Muslim civilizations. This education
is a first step towards building dialogue and understanding.
The effort I am describing will have to be systematic and
extended over many decades to be successful. It must reach
a wide spectrum of students in secondary schools and not be
restricted to the specialized knowledge of higher education
as it is today. In this regard, I applaud the initiative the German government has made in introducing material about
Islam into the public education curriculum.

As a Muslim, I accept that such a truly comprehensive
effort is likely to cause unwelcoming reactions from a large
number of forces in the Judeo-Christian world. Relations
between this world and the world of Islam historically have
been conditioned by interfaith attitudes. These were vividly
and brutally illustrated at the time of the Crusades. Then,
the issues were focussed upon which faith was best placed

to redeem the individual soul. Proselytization was probably the single most powerful driving force.

In recent decades, interfaith dialogue has been occurring in numerous countries. Unfortunately, every time the word "faith" is used in such a context, there is an inherent supposition that the issue of proselytization is lurking at the side. But faith, after all, is only one aspect of human society. We must approach this issue today within the dimension of civilizations learning about each other and speaking to each other, not exclusively through the more narrow focus of interfaith dialectic. Such an approach would also be immensely beneficial to the Muslim world. It would result in its much greater emphasis on learning about the pluralism and richness of its own history and about the diversity of the countries, cultures, religious institutions and interpretations of Islam. Learning must not be restricted, as it often is, to matters of theology.

Today, theological interpretation and proselytization continue to divide among Catholic, Orthodox and Protestant interpretations in the Christian world, as they do in the Islamic world between Sunni and Shia and their various subdivisions. I would hope to see the day when the definition of an educated person in Judeo-Christian culture would include an intelligent understanding of the Muslim world. That person would appreciate the eminent position of Islamic civilizations in human thought and knowledge, including an understanding of the tradition in those civilizations of research and achievements, from philosophy and the arts to the sciences, architecture and engineering.

The current void of knowledge makes it impossible to establish a dialogue, because you cannot build a dialogue based upon ignorance. With whom do you have dialogue? Without meaningful dialogue, you cannot construct coherent and sustainable foreign policy, because you will not have the ability to predict. You will not understand the forces at play. How would the handling of the situations in Kashmir, Afghanistan, Iraq and the wider Middle East, or the Philippines have been different if the main players had benefited from a thorough understanding of the history and culture of those regions?

Let me turn now to civil society. None of the initiatives I have discussed can be effective in the absence of a robust civil society, which is critical to supporting pluralism and ultimately effective democracies. Civil society includes charitable organizations and NGOs. It also encompasses organizations charged with maintaining best practices, such as legal societies and associations of accountants, doctors and engineers. It includes trade associations, unions and journalist groups. Village organizations, women's groups, microcredit entities and agricultural cooperatives are important components as well. Some organizations are primarily urban, others primarily rural, while still others provide links and support to both urban and rural environments.

Civil society makes an enormous contribution to human development, filling the gaps between government, the business sector and the family. It does things the state cannot and thus supports citizens in nation building. Most important, civil society underwrites human progress. It acts as a stabilizer or buttress in times of economic slowdown or social stress. When democracies are failing, or have failed, it is the institutions of civil society that can carry an added burden to help sustain improvements in quality of life.

In his Munich remarks, Minister Fischer recognized the importance of partnerships in building the indigenous capacity of civil society in developing countries. I whole-heartedly welcome the principle of partnerships. Civil society institutions in developing nations must have expert assistance if they are to be a bulwark for democratic pro-cesses and play a role in helping people improve their living conditions. Partnerships can take many forms. They include the twinning of institutions, the secondment of experts in education and health care and the provision of continuing education for practitioners in fields such as nursing, journal-ism and the charitable and not-for-profit sectors.

Germany and the AKDN already collaborate on a wide and expanding scale in areas of risk and sensitivity such as Pakistan, Afghanistan and Central Asia. Through a great variety of village and community organizations, we encour-age people to overcome their antagonisms and work together to find solutions to common problems in the search for a better life.

Northern Pakistan is an excellent example of how this support for civil society and pluralism can buttress democ-racy. We have been working in that isolated region for more than twenty years, with German participation since 1992. Some 3,900 village-based organizations have been created, dealing with a range of issues from women's initiatives and water usage to savings and credit. Economic growth has been impressive, and hostilities born of despair have been replaced by cooperation and hope for the future. In recent local elections, many leaders of these village-based organizations sought and achieved elected positions. The lesson here is that democracy can succeed even in the most remote rural areas, where much of our vital work is concentrated, if one is patient and works to build up indigenous capacity.

The AKDN has begun to formalize its support for democracy, pluralism and civil society by establishing a Global Centre for Pluralism in Ottawa. This education and research centre will work closely with governments, academia and civil society to foster legislation and policy to strengthen local capacity for enhancing pluralism. We would welcome the participation of the German government in helping transport the fruits of this venture to the developing world. I have the hope and the confidence that our partnerships will continue and be characterized by a willingness to innovate, to take risks for great reward and to have the patience and determination for the long-term commitment required.

All of you assembled here have the ability to shape the future direction of the world for the better. Each of you, in your role in diplomacy, may reflect upon how the issues I have identified might help in addressing, in a strategic way, the kaleidoscope of changing patterns in the regions and areas of responsibility in which you work.

Is sustaining democracy a serious issue in our quest to transform developing nations into peaceful and productive modern societies? How can we nurture and support the growth of civil society? What are the educational and cultural approaches that can support greater pluralism, understanding and dialogue? And finally, by responding to these issues, can we reduce risk and increase the probability of success in helping the people of the developing world to attain a better life?

REFERENCE

Fischer, Joschka. Minister for Foreign Affairs and Vice Chancellor, Federal Republic of Germany. "Speech on the 40th Munich Conference on Security Policy." Address to the fortieth Munich Conference on Security Policy, Munich, Germany, February 7, 2004.

ARCHITECTURE
AS A FORCE FOR CHANGE

NINTH AWARD CYCLE *of the*
AGA KHAN AWARD *for* ARCHITECTURE

New Delhi, India, November 27, 2004

THE RECOGNITION WE are giving tonight carries the name "Award for Architecture." But it represents much more. The Award recognizes the efforts of architects and their clients, builders large and small, governments, planners, international organizations, granting agencies, village organizations and individuals. All of them are collectively responsible for creating a humane and socially supportive built environment that is so important to our quality of life.

It is therefore most appropriate that this event is taking place in India, a country rich in cultural heritage and pluralistic traditions. Here, many cultures have maintained their distinct identities while combining and cooperating to create something even greater, the dynamic and vibrant India of the modern world. This is also a country where the struggle for social justice and an improved quality of life has made tremendous strides over many decades through the continuous efforts of governments and civil society. This year's Award recognizes projects that cover the entire spectrum of human capability and human need. The striking differences in these award winners reflect the enormous range of need for human habitat that must be met in the world today.

It is now twenty-seven years since the Award was launched. At that time, I was becoming increasingly disturbed by the loss of cultural identity and appropriateness in the architecture and built environments of much of the Muslim world. A few centuries ago, architecture was one of the great forms of artistic expression in the many diverse Muslim societies. It permeated all types of buildings and spaces, both secular and religious, rural and urban, in the multiple Islamic cultures spread across the world and in neighbouring non-Muslim societies as well.

The magnificent structure built to honour the second Mughal emperor, Humayun, is one of the early examples of the spectacular architectural legacy the Mughals left to the people of the subcontinent. The Taj Mahal, built almost a hundred years later, is one of the world's most admired buildings of all time. Before these, the early Muslims had made their distinctive architectural mark in Syria, Iraq, Fatimid Egypt, Spain, Persia and Anatolia. But in recent years, Islamic architecture seemed to have lost its identity—I should perhaps say identities—and its inspiration. Occasionally, construction tended to repeat previous Islamic styles. But much more often, it simply absorbed imported architectural forms, language and materials.

There were several reasons for this. In part, modernity, equated with all that was Western, had come to be seen as representing improved quality. And most Muslim architects were trained in Western schools and had little knowledge or understanding of the traditions of Islamic architecture. The net result was that our cities, villages and rural areas were being transformed by the insidious introduction and expansion of inappropriate, irrelevant architecture and planning.

In Islam, the Holy Quran says that man is God's noblest creation, to whom He has entrusted the stewardship of all that is on earth. Each generation must leave for its successors an enhanced and sustainable social and physical environment. I am sure every responsible citizen in every part of the world would share this aspiration. Therefore, we set out on a long journey to try to understand the causes of this sad situation, which Muslim and non-Muslim architects alike recognized as unfortunate, but which none knew how to alter. Some of the most eminent architects and men and women of different disciplines and cultures joined me in this endeavour, to understand the causes of this decline in quality and design. The enormity of the challenge caused many to doubt that a significant result could be achieved. It seemed certain that decades would pass before results, if any, would be seen.

The evolution of the Award has been, first, engaging constituencies to develop consensus about the nature of the problem; second, developing the means to support change, and finally, exposing solutions to the many who are involved in the process of developing human habitat.

Now, as we enter our second quarter-century of the Aga Khan Award for Architecture, we might ask ourselves: are the lessons we have learned in this particular cultural endeavour applicable to other environments and other cultural traditions that are stagnating or under threat?

I, of course, start with the basic assumption that the world is a much better place because it is pluralist and multicultural. Imagine what it would be like living in a world of no diversity, a world where we were all the same colour, shape and size, ate the same biryani, told the same jokes and combed our hair identically. Aside from the fact that my comb, sadly, serves less purpose these days, I would find a world like that quite boring. I am therefore convinced that supporting diversity and cultures under threat is a worthwhile and fruitful venture.

This leads me to the fundamental question we sought to answer in establishing these awards. It is one that I think is applicable to any initiative aimed at nurturing and supporting cultures at risk: how do we protect the past and inspire the future? Put another way, how do we reshape and reposition knowledge, taste and appreciation in the public psyche, and among those who play a role in developing human habitat?

From the beginning, we knew that to have a realistic chance of bringing about fundamental and lasting change, we had to reach out and raise awareness, not just among architects but among clients, corporations, governments, planners, educators and financiers. That meant we needed to build an all-encompassing profile of people and habitat, not only in the Islamic world but in countries where Muslims live and interact with other communities, both urban and rural. We broadened the definition of architecture from one that tended to look only at individual structures to one that encompassed entire neighbourhoods, including informal settlements, village communities and open public spaces. In the first nine cycles, some 2,661 projects have been assessed and documented in eighty-eight countries, an unparalleled data resource base. The independent master juries have recognized ninety-seven projects in twenty-five countries. These projects demonstrate widely different aspects of architectural solutions that affect quality of life, ranging from the restoration of historic urban fabrics and monuments to the reforestation of a university campus of over three hundred hectares. They have included generic models of individual houses and modest individual efforts, large civic complexes and high-tech, ultra-modern buildings that set new trends for the future.

Another important step in the process was to promote awareness and understanding of appropriate technologies and solutions. The Muslim world is multicultural, is diverse in geography, terrain and climate, and exhibits extremes of wealth and poverty. This diversity required us to be sensitive not only to local needs but to the local capacity and resources available to meet those needs.

And finally, new initiatives outside the Award itself became necessary. In education, our Trust for Culture supports the Aga Khan Program in Islamic Architecture at Harvard and M.I.T. The Trust's Historic Cities Support

Programme helps create new examples and models for reviving historic buildings and spaces.

Our efforts have been richly rewarded in the growth of knowledge and awareness of Islamic architecture and landscaping in educational bodies around the world. In the most eminent Western schools, there is a much greater academic offering and commitment to the field of Islamic architecture. In Muslim countries, we have seen the birth of new schools and a new generation of architectural teachers and scholars. Most important, we are getting better habitat. I think that the Award and the cluster of initiatives born from it are truly protecting the past and inspiring the future.

But although we can be pleased with this progress, there is much more to be done. Quality housing remains the most essential need for societies everywhere, in both rural and urban environments. Industrial facilities and workplaces are not at a level of excellence that makes them exceptional. Rapidly expanding urban centres throughout the world lack public parks and open spaces. Too few solutions are emerging to address problems of transport, congestion and pollution. The growth of slums, the consequence of the relentless forces of urbanization, has not been stopped or even slowed down. And although many fine examples of rural projects have been represented in past Award cycles, still there are not enough. We have much yet to strive for. But I believe the process we have launched has become a self-sustaining and unstoppable force for change in human habitat not only in the Muslim world but in much of the developing world as well.

The larger and perhaps more interesting question is whether this approach might be adopted to support other cultures that are at risk. The issues we have been attempting to address through the process of the Aga Khan Award for Architecture are not exclusive to the Muslim world. The non-Muslim world struggles equally with explosive population growth, poverty, environmental degradation, exodus from rural areas, globalization and the impact on cultural identity of new forms of media. I hope that the lessons learned in the process we have established are applicable to the many others in similar circumstances. Perhaps these lessons will one day be seen as an important contribution from the Muslim world: a contribution to the broader cause of maintaining and enhancing a multicultural, pluralist world and a responsive, appropriate human habitat.

top: His Highness talks with graduates at the convocation ceremonies of the Aga Khan University, Karachi, Pakistan, on November 19, 1994. The University celebrated its tenth anniversary that year. GARY OTTE/AKDN

bottom: His Highness at the Aga Khan University convocation ceremony with graduates of the School of Nursing, Karachi, Pakistan, November 19, 1994.

above: His Highness and local dignitaries walk through historic Stone Town on the island of Zanzibar, Tanzania, on July 18, 1991. Since 1988, the Aga Khan Development Network has supported the social, economic and cultural revitalization of Zanzibar, including through projects related to the Stone Town Cultural Centre, the Zanzibar Serena Inn and Kelele Square. GARY OTTE/AKDN

facing page, top: His Highness at a ceremony held in Gouvieux, France, on July 11, 2007, to mark the fiftieth anniversary of his accession to the Ismaili Imamat. ZAHUR RAMJI/AKDN

facing page, bottom: His Highness speaks to villagers of Natugo, in a remote area of Mozambique's Cabo Delgado province, in November 2007. On his right is Lebreton Saah Nyambe, director of the Coastal Rural Support Programme, an initiative designed to support the development efforts of the local population. GARY OTTE/AKDN

above: His Highness (*centre*) and Ahmed Mohamed Ag Hamani (*right*), the prime minister of Mali, meet with the Imam, Mr. Abdramane ben Essayouti (*left*), and local dignitaries at the fourteenth-century Djingereiber Mosque, Timbuktu, in October 2003. GARY OTTE/AKDN

facing page, top: His Highness visits Al-Azhar Park during the early phases of construction in March 1997. The project involved excavating and restoring the adjoining twelfth-century Ayyubid wall, rehabilitating monuments and buildings in the neighbouring district of Darb al-Ahmar and implementing an extensive social development program. ZAHUR RAMJI/AKDN

facing page, bottom: His Highness greets restoration technicians at the Tarabay Mausoleum, part of an ambitious project to revitalize the impoverished district of Darb al-Ahmar in historic Cairo, in October 2007. GARY OTTE/AKDN

top: His Highness meets students at the Aga Khan Academy in Mombasa, Kenya, on November 14, 2006. The Academy is one of a network of institutions created to offer education of an international standard of excellence in Asia and Africa. GARY OTTE/AKDN

bottom: His Highness and Hamid Karzai, then chairman of the Interim Administration of Afghanistan, at the March 23, 2002, launch of the "Back to School" initiative led by UNICEF in Kabul. The Aga Khan was in Afghanistan to sign the Agreement of Cooperation for Development that established an operating framework for the Aga Khan Development Network in that country. GARY OTTE/AKDN

top: His Highness meets with Prime Minister Manmohan Singh in New Delhi, India, in November 2004. The Aga Khan was in India to announce the winners of the ninth cycle of the Aga Khan Award for Architecture. GARY OTTE/AKDN

bottom: Their Excellencies Governor General Adrienne Clarkson (*centre*) and Mr. John Ralston Saul (*left*) stroll with His Highness at Rideau Hall, Ottawa, in June 2005. On the occasion of this visit, the Aga Khan was invested as an honorary Companion of the Order of Canada in recognition of his lifetime of outstanding achievement, dedication to the community and service to the nation. ZAHUR RAMJI/AKDN

left: His Highness visits a project in Sost, in the Northern Areas of Pakistan, in November 1987. The Aga Khan Rural Support Programme worked with local village organizations to construct irrigation channels along the vertical, rocky slopes of the Karakoram Mountains. GARY OTTE/AKDN

below: His Highness meets with nurse-midwives at the Bamiyan Hospital in northern Afghanistan in November 2005. Training health care professionals, particularly women, is part of the AKDN's efforts, with the cooperation of the government of Afghanistan, to rebuild the country's health system. GARY OTTE/AKDN

DEMOCRACY, PLURALISM
AND CIVIL SOCIETY

NOBEL INSTITUTE

Oslo, Norway, April 7, 2005

I AM PARTICULARLY HONOURED to be speaking at the Nobel Institute, respected worldwide for its promotion and recognition of exceptional endeavours to reduce human conflict. It is also a rare privilege to address such a learned and experienced audience, which includes not only officials in government charged with issues of human development but also leaders of Norwegian civil society who are important partners in Norway's impressive international development efforts.

In my remarks today, I will pose to you several questions that I will attempt to go some way towards answering. First, why are so many democracies failing in Asia and Africa? Second, is enough being done to help these young countries achieve successful forms of democratic governance? Third, are there common factors causing this failure of democracies? Fourth, why is the international community unable to get engaged at the early stages before crisis occurs? And finally, what can be done?

Before I begin, perhaps I can give you some background on my perspective. My role in human development stems from my position as Imam, or spiritual leader, of the Shia Ismaili Muslims, as designated by my grandfather in 1957. In all interpretations of Islam, Imams, whether they are Shia or Sunni, are required not only to lead in the interpretation of the faith but equally to contribute to improving the quality of life of the people who refer to them. This dual obligation is often difficult to appreciate from the viewpoint of Christian interpretations of the role that church leaders are expected to perform. It is on this ethical premise, which bridges faith and society, that I established the Aga Khan Development Network. Its multiple agencies and programs have long been active in many areas of Africa and Asia that are home to some of the poorest and most diverse populations in the world, serving people without regard to their ethnicity, gender or faith.

The community I lead of Shia Ismaili Muslims is culturally, ethnically and linguistically very diverse. Their main concentration is in South and Central Asia, the Middle East and sub-Saharan Africa. In recent decades the community has also established a substantial presence in North America and western Europe. We have lived through colonialism and independence, two World Wars, the Cold War, and many local and regional wars. We have seen the collapse of the Soviet Union and the birth of new states. The pendulum has swung from private ownership to nationalization and back to privatization. And we have lived in democracy and under dictatorship.

The community and its institutions are in many ways a microcosm of the last century in the developing world, and we have learned many lessons. I put it to you that no human development initiative can be sustainable unless we are successful in achieving three essential conditions. We must operate in an environment that invests in, rather than seeks to stifle, pluralism and diversity. We must have an extensive, engaged civil society. And we must have stable, competent democratic governance. These three conditions are mutually reinforcing. Taken together, they allow developing societies gradually to become masters of the process and to make that process self-sustainable.

The effective world of the future will be one of pluralism, a world that understands, appreciates and builds on diversity. The rejection of pluralism plays a significant role in breeding destructive conflicts, from which no continent has been spared in recent decades. But pluralist societies are not accidents of history. They are a product of enlightened education and continuous investment by governments and all of civil society in recognizing and celebrating the diversity of the world's peoples.

What is being done to support this key value for society and for democracy in Asia and Africa, to pre-empt catastrophe rather than simply respond to it? The Aga Khan Development Network intends to help create some permanent institutional capacity to address this critical issue through a Global Centre for Pluralism. It will be based in

Ottawa, to draw from Canada's successful record in constructing and sustaining pluralist civil society. The centre will work closely with governments and with academia and civil society around the world. It will seek to foster legislation and policy to strengthen developing countries' capacity for enhancing pluralism in all spheres of modern life, including law, justice, the arts, the media, financial services, health and education. I believe leadership everywhere must continuously work to ensure that pluralism, and all its benefits, become top global priorities.

In this effort, civil society has a vital role. By its very nature, civil society is pluralist, because it seeks to speak for the multiple interests not represented by the state. I refer, for example, to organizations that ensure best practices, such as legal societies and associations of accountants, doctors and engineers. The meritocracy they represent is the very foundation of pluralism. And meritocracy is one of the principles of democracy itself. Village organizations, women's and student groups, microcredit entities and agricultural cooperatives help give access and voice to those who often are disenfranchised. Journalist associations also play a key role, by explaining the political process, guarding against corruption and keeping governments accountable. Responsible reporting and competent comment on critical issues, and on the hard choices that society must address, are essential elements in the functioning of a democracy. Civil society organizations make a major contribution to human development, particularly when democracies are failing or have failed, for it is then that the institutions of civil society can, and often do, carry an added burden to help sustain improvements in quality of life.

I believe strongly that a critical part of any development strategy should include support for civil society. I know that Norway supports this approach and works actively with its own civil society organizations to build capacity in the developing world. Twinning civil society institutions is a promising approach, to which the Aga Khan Development Network institutions and programs are very receptive.

Let me turn now to the question of democratic governance. If we were to look at a map of the world charting armed conflicts in the last fifteen years, it would show that nearly two-thirds have occurred in the developing countries of Asia and Africa. More than 80 per cent were internal conflicts, either full-blown civil wars or state-sanctioned aggression against minorities in those countries. In nearly every instance, these internal conflicts were predictable because they were the culmination of a gradual deterioration in pluralist, inclusive governance. In too many cases—and I can speak here of our experiences in Uganda, Bangladesh, Tajikistan and Afghanistan—this sad but foreseeable turn of events has had severely adverse effects lasting more than a generation.

The question I have is this: If these breakdowns in governance were predictable, why was the international community powerless to get engaged at the early stages, to help arrest the deterioration and prevent the suffering that resulted? Second, are there common factors in the majority of these situations that we have not fully recognized?

I suggest to you a major problem is that the industrialized world is too often severely lacking in credible information about the forces at play in the developing world. Take as an example the phrase "clash of civilizations," which has travelled far and wide. I have said many times previously, and I would like today to reaffirm my conviction, that what we have been observing in recent decades is not a clash of civilizations but a clash of ignorance. This ignorance is both historic and of our time. This is not the occasion to analyze the historic causes of the deep ignorance that exists between the Judeo-Christian and Muslim worlds. But I am convinced many of today's problems could have been avoided if there had been better understanding and more serious dialogue between the two.

The issue of ignorance, or lack of solid information, and its impact on our world today is illustrated by events in Iraq. No less deplorable is that the 9/11 attack on the United States was a direct consequence of the international community ignoring the human tragedy that was Afghanistan at that time. Both the Afghan and the Iraqi situations were driven by the lack of precise information and understanding. My fundamental point is this: since the collapse of the Cold War, the need has grown exponentially for the world's leaders to be able to understand, and properly predict, what is likely to happen in parts of the world in which they previously had no reason to be involved. The task of addressing this need cannot be met by the resources presently being engaged.

I note that Norway's Minister of Foreign Affairs, Jan Petersen, spoke of this very problem just last week in Beijing.

He called for the international community to provide fragile states with assistance in governance that is, and I quote, "more systematic, more strategic, more persevering and more reliable." My suggestion is to examine this question in depth.

Let me share with you some real-world field examples. Just as we read about the supposed clash of civilizations, we read about so-called failed states. In fact, at least in my definition, a state cannot fail. What we are observing in reality is the massive failure of democracy around the world. I estimate that some 40 per cent of the states of the United Nations are failed democracies. Depending upon the definitions applied, between 450 million and 900 million people currently live in countries under severe or moderate stress as a result of these failures. To me, therefore, a central question is why these democracies are failing. What can the world's nations and international organizations do to sustain their competence and stability? Let me now illustrate some specific issues that I believe are contributing to this fragility.

A number of countries in which the Aga Khan Development Network is active have opted to harness enormous resources to universal primary education, causing a significant underexpenditure on secondary and tertiary education. This educational policy originated from a number of ill-advised social economists in the early 1960s. The degradation of secondary and tertiary education is not a new phenomenon. It is being made significantly worse today, however, by the lack of educational resources available to secondary and tertiary students who, after all, represent the leaders of tomorrow.

Second, if governance is a science, as I believe it is, developing countries must educate about governance at the secondary and tertiary levels. Otherwise, they deprive their intelligentsia of academic grounding in the critical knowledge of how democratic states operate. A survey today in secondary schools or universities in Africa or Asia would find that "government," as a subject in its own right, is either nonexistent or given low priority.

It is clear that over the next decades, a large number of countries will be designing new constitutions or refining existing ones. New regional groupings will come into place. Many young democracies will spawn new political structures. But where are the men and women who will lead? Just as education in governance is weak, the developing world continues to suffer from insufficient support to certain liberal professions that are critical to democracy. In my experience, the teaching profession and journalism are failing to attract the level of men and women who are essential for these professions to make their appropriate contribution to democracy. The challenge is therefore clear. We must create the human and institutional resources to build and sustain young democracies.

As long as the developed world hesitates to commit long-term investment towards education for democracy, and instead laments the issue of so-called failed states, much of the developing world will continue to face bleak prospects for democracy. And the West should not discount that an accumulation of failed democracies could be a serious threat to itself and its values, capable of causing, if not conflict, deep undercurrents of stress among societies. What seems apparent today is that the developed world must find the resources to provide consistent and meaningful assistance to fragile states struggling with democratic governance. The world cannot sit by while countries spiral into crisis.

Some of the things we can do, I suggest to you, are as follows: We must make a greater commitment to build capacity in the developing world to teach the science of government. We must make an aggressive effort to support indigenous civil society, both to assist in the building of democracies and to provide a buttress in times of stress. We must provide active encouragement and support for pluralism. Above all, we must set about to improve knowledge and understanding of the factors in the developing world that are encouraging— or undermining—democratic governance.

THE BRIDGES THAT UNITE US

FOUNDATION CEREMONY *of the*
DELEGATION *of the* ISMAILI IMAMAT

Ottawa, Canada, June 6, 2005

NEARLY THREE AND a half decades ago, Canada opened her
shores to dispossessed thousands—Ismailis and others—who had been expelled from their homeland, Uganda,
which was then in the grip of a brutal tyranny. Many, from
such distressed lands as Afghanistan and Tajikistan, have
also found here a welcome home. With industry, intelligence, education and self-help, but above all with all the
reassurances that a just, pluralist society bestows, they were
able rapidly to rebuild their lives and institutions, and they
are discharging their responsibilities as citizens of this great
land and to the less privileged elsewhere. Today's occasion is
therefore an appropriate opportunity to renew, on behalf of
the Ismaili community and myself as their Imam, our lasting gratitude to the government and people of Canada.

The event that brings us together, the initiation of the Delegation of the Ismaili Imamat, is a celebration of the Ismaili community's permanent presence in and commitment to Canada. Reflecting the pluralism of the Muslim world generally, the Ismailis are a richly diverse community within the Shia branch of Islam and belong to distinct ethnogeographic and linguistic traditions, namely Arab, Iranian, Central Asian, Chinese and South Asian. They live across Asia, the Middle East and sub-Saharan Africa, while in recent decades they have also established a substantial presence in North America and Europe.

The Ismailis are thus a transnational community and are, first and foremost, active and loyal citizens of the countries where they live, although in outlook they transcend the divisions of north and south, east and west. Whatever the context of their lives, they all share, like other Muslims, the commitment to an ethic whose values converge on the inherent dignity of the human person as the noblest of creation. Historically, Ismailis are united by a common allegiance to the living hereditary Imam of the time in the progeny of Islam's last and final Prophet Muhammad (may peace be upon him) through his daughter, Fatima, and her husband, Hazrat Ali, the Prophet's cousin and the first Shia Imam. In the Muslim ethical tradition, which links spirit and matter, the Imam leads not only in the interpretation of the faith but also in the effort to improve the quality of life of his community and of the wider societies within which that community lives. A guiding principle of the Imamat's institutions is to replace walls that divide with bridges that unite.

The Delegation in the city of Ottawa will serve a representational role for the Imamat and the non-denominational, philanthropic and development agencies that constitute the Aga Khan Development Network. An open, secular facility, the Delegation will be a sanctuary for peaceful, quiet diplomacy, informed by the Imamat's outlook of global convergence and the development of civil society. It will be an enabling venue for fruitful public engagements, information services and educational programs, all backed up by high-quality research to sustain a vibrant intellectual centre and a key policy-informing institution.

The architectural planning has been entrusted to the capable hands of Fumihiko Maki, an architect of world standing. Maki and Associates have my enthusiastic admiration for addressing, with tact and empathy, challenges of design that are difficult and subtle. They call for translating concepts that have a context in our faith and our history, yet stride boldly and confidently ahead into modernity; for expressing both the exoteric and the esoteric as well as our awe and humility towards the mysteries of nature, time and beyond. The outcome is an interplay of multiple facets, like rock crystal. In it are platforms of pure but translucent horizontality. Light's full spectrum comes alive and disappears as the eye moves. In Islam, the Divine is reflected in nature's creation.

The building will rest on a solid linear granite podium. Above it will be a glass dome through which light will illuminate, from multiple directions, two symbolic spaces: an interior atrium and an exterior courtyard landscaped in

four quarters, recalling the traditional Persian-Islamic garden, the *chahar-bagh*. Nature, through the greenery of trees
and flowers, will be on the site but also in the building, just
as we are sometimes able to see leaves and petals that are
captured in rock crystal but still visible through its unique
translucency. The building will be a metaphor for human-
ism and enlightenment and for the humility that comes
from the constant search for answers that leads inevitably to
more questions.

The Delegation, with its openness and transparency,
will be a symbolic seat for the Imamat's permanent presence in Canada and a platform for constructive exchanges
that mutually broaden moral and intellectual horizons. It
will be a window for the AKDN to reinforce existing, and
cultivate new, partnerships with national and international
agencies present in Ottawa that share the ethic of contributing to an improved quality of life in the developing world.
This concern to improve the human condition underlines
the long-standing relationship of the Ismaili Imamat and
the AKDN with Canada's government and civil society institutions in many parts of Africa and Asia. Our presence in
these areas, home to some of the most disadvantaged and
diverse populations in the world, has exposed us jointly to
a realistic appreciation of the problems of persistent under-
development, namely that human progress can only be
sustained when people are able to participate in their own
governance. Parliamentary elections are only one aspect of
participation. Equally, or perhaps more, important is the
access to a healthy, multifaceted civil society pervading all

areas of human interaction, rural and urban, able to seek out and harness the best from all segments of the population.

Successful experience with democracy, civil society and pluralism are the national genius of Canada, of which much of the developing world is in dire need. As an example—and there are many—of how these Canadian assets can help transform living conditions, I often cite our experience in Northern Pakistan, a case-study situation of poor development prospects in a harsh, sparsely endowed physical environment further beset by ethnic and religious hostilities. The AKDN has been present there for over twenty years, with CIDA, the Canadian International Development Agency, as a lead partner. Our joint micro-experiment with grassroots democracy, civil society and pluralism has been the springboard for a dramatic trebling of per capita incomes, with corresponding improvements in social services and cultural awareness in what was once one of the poorest areas on earth. Tensions occasionally resurface, incited by mischief. But by and large, where once there was conflict born of despair and past memories, there is now a spirit of consensus built around hope for the future. This is, therefore, a good opportunity to acknowledge gratefully Canada's intellectual, institutional and financial contribution to a partnership with the AKDN in the creation of the new Global Centre for Pluralism here in Ottawa. A tribute to, and drawing on, Canada's experience of pluralist democracy, this research and education centre will work closely with governments, academia and civil society in culturally diverse countries. The aim will be to foster policy and legislation that enables pluralism to take root in all spheres of modern life: law, justice, the arts, media, financial services, health and education.

It is heartening that, in a report of March this year, Canada's Standing Committee on Foreign Affairs and International Trade recognized the critical importance of developing partnerships with the countries of the Muslim world. It stressed the need to work not only with their governments but also with civil society and minorities in realizing Canada's key international policy objectives of sharing its experience of good governance and economic development. Acknowledging the contribution of Muslim civilization to the West's own development, and Islam's affinity to the values of pluralism and liberal democratic principles, the committee and the government have signalled their intention to take steps to improve mutual understanding between Canada and the Muslim world.

The Delegation of the Ismaili Imamat in the federal capital and the new Aga Khan Museum and Ismaili Centre to be built in Toronto are symbols of the seriousness and respect that Canada, leading the West generally, accords to the world of Islam, of which the Ismaili community, though a diverse minority itself, is fully representative. May this mutual understanding, so important to the future stability and progress of our world, flourish manyfold. It is my sincere hope that, by its presence and the functions it fulfills, the Delegation of the Ismaili Imamat will be an illuminating landmark on Sussex Drive. An epitome of friendship to one and all, it will radiate Islam's precepts of one humanity, the dignity of man, and the nobility of joint striving in deeds of goodness.

REFERENCE

Canada. "Exploring Canada's Relations with the Countries of the Muslim World." Committee Chair: Bernard Patry. (Ottawa: Standing Committee on Foreign Affairs and International Trade, 2004). http://cmte.parl.gc.ca/Content/HOC/committee/373/fait/reports/rp1281987/faitrp01/faitrp01-e.pdf.

WHAT MAKES DEMOCRACY WORK?

"COSMOPOLITAN SOCIETY, HUMAN SAFETY,
and RIGHTS *in* PLURAL *and* PEACEFUL SOCIETIES,"
EVORA UNIVERSITY SYMPOSIUM

Evora, Portugal, February 12, 2006

IT IS A great honour to be invited to address this esteemed
audience on such a relevant topic. Our symposium title
speaks of societies that are at once plural and peaceful—a
goal that is important but also elusive. Even our best efforts
to combine stability with modernity seem to be constantly
disrupted. Some of these disruptions come from new technologies, from Internet blogs to biogenetics. Others spring
from nature, from changing weather patterns or mutating
viruses. Still others arise from social transformations such
as new patterns of family life and enormous migrations of
people.

Newspaper headlines remind us daily of growing strains
and stresses: civil disorder in places as affluent as France and
Australia; the plight of hurricane victims in Louisiana and

earthquake victims in Kashmir; the uses of nuclear energy; the sense of impotence amid suffering in places like Darfur. The planet becomes more crowded and its resources less abundant. The gap widens between rich and poor. People everywhere cry out against these evils. But change, when it comes at all, is painfully slow, and we sometimes seem to be sliding backward.

I should also mention the headlines of this past week, which chart the widening gulf between Islamic and Western societies. Here the culprit has not been military action or diplomatic failure but the power of media images— deeply offensive caricatures—that have profoundly offended one billion four hundred million Muslims around the world, including myself. The question I ask as I read all these headlines is this: why are political and civil leaders, in rich and poor nations alike, unable to develop the vision and harness the will to confront such challenges more effectively?

What makes this sense of impasse especially disturbing is that it so often represents a failure of democracy. For many centuries, it was the conviction of enlightened people that societies would truly come to grips with their problems once they became democratic. The great barrier to progress, these people said, was that governments listened to the special few, rather than to the voice of the many. If we could only advance the march of democracy, they argued, then a progressive agenda would inevitably fall into place.

But I am not sure that such an analysis holds up any longer. For the past half century, we have seen great waves of ostensibly democratic reform, from the fading of colonialism in the mid-twentieth century to the fall of the Iron Curtain. But despite this apparent progress, the results have often been disappointing. I can scarcely count, nor fully catalogue, the variety of governments I have visited over the past five decades, from the most autocratic to the most participatory. Often, the more democratic governments were the more effective and responsible. But this was not consistently true, and I have recently found it to be decreasingly true. In fact, nearly 40 per cent of UN member nations are now categorized as "failed democracies."

Democracy and progress do not always go hand in hand, and the growing threat of "failed states" can often be described as the failure of democracy. Frequently, democratic failures grow out of sheer incompetence. Publics are asked to vote on issues that bewilder them. Candidates obscure their own views and distort their opponents' positions. Journalists transmit superficial rhetoric and slight underlying realities. People are appointed to jobs they cannot do but are rarely held accountable. Corruption for some becomes a way of life. Meanwhile, the media tell audiences what they want to know rather than what they ought to know. And what too many people want today is not to be informed but to be entertained.

The breakdowns are institutional as well as personal. Democratic systems veer between too many checks and balances and too few. Parliaments, in particular, often lack the expertise and structure to grapple with complex problems, and they are often too factionalized or too subservient to sustain a coherent view. For all these reasons, democracies often make bad decisions. And when democracies are ineffective, disenchanted publics are tempted in other directions. Latin America is one place where democracy was thought to be expanding in recent years. Yet the UN Development Program reports that 55 per cent of those surveyed in eighteen Latin American countries would support authoritarian rule if it brought economic progress. The challenge of democratic competence, then, is a central problem of our time. Meeting that challenge must be one of our central callings.

Another development, which is mentioned in the title of this symposium, has vastly compounded the challenge of democratic renewal. I refer to the rapid proliferation of cosmopolitan populations. The world is becoming more pluralist in fact but it is not keeping pace in spirit. Cosmopolitan social patterns have not yet been matched by what I would call "a cosmopolitan ethic."

Peoples mix and mingle, side by side, to an extent that was once unimaginable. Waves of migration indelibly change the rhythms, colours and flavours of their host communities. Some 150 million legal immigrants live outside their country of birth, joined by uncounted millions who have immigrated illegally. These trends will continue. Globalization has dissolved the tight bond between community and geography. Economic opportunity—for rich and poor alike—can lie in distant lands. Some 45 million young people enter the job market in the developing world each year, but there are not enough jobs at home for all of them. Meanwhile, war and civil conflict add their refugees to the mix.

Immigration brings both blessings and problems. Immigrants now account for two-thirds of the population growth in the thirty member countries of the OECD (Organisation for Economic Co-operation and Development), where an aging workforce requires new young workers. Meanwhile, remittances sent home by immigrants total some $145 billion a year and generate nearly $300 billion in economic activity—more than either foreign development aid or foreign direct investment provides. At the same time, immigrant communities can sharply strain public and private resources. The resulting competition with older residents can cause resentment and hostility. More than half of the respondents in various European opinion polls have a negative view of immigration.

The so-called clash of civilizations is both a local and a global danger. But it need not be this way. Nor has it always been this way down through the sweep of history. Yes, cultural clash has been one major theme in the human story. But so has intercultural cooperation. This country and this university know from your own history how Islamic and Christian cultures met in this part of the world many centuries ago and how enriching their interactions were for both traditions. This is a good time and place to emphasize the manifold blessings that come when peoples decide to stop shouting at one another and instead begin listening and learning.

Cross-cultural interaction has been a central focus of my own activities in the nearly fifty years since I became Imam of the Shia Ismaili Muslims. The ethics of Islam bridge faith and society, so my responsibilities as spiritual leader are accompanied by a strong engagement in issues of community well-being. The Ismailis are themselves a culturally diverse community. They live as minorities in more than twenty-five countries, primarily in the developing world, but also in Europe, including Portugal, and North America. This Ismaili multicultural experience is reflected in the approach of the Aga Khan Development Network, working with a wide array of partners to help the disadvantaged, regardless of their origin. We are pleased, for example, that our work in Portugal has recently been formalized in cooperative agreements with both the Portuguese government and the Patriarchate of Lisbon. In discussing cultural diversity, let me also mention our recent partnership with the Government of Canada to create a new Global Centre for Pluralism in Ottawa. This centre will draw on both Ismaili experience and the experience of Canada itself, where a pluralist society thrives and where—in contrast to much of world opinion—80 per cent of the public welcomes immigration as a positive development.

In honouring me today, you honour the tradition I represent. In doing so, you are renewing an inspiring story of intercultural affection and intercultural respect, of mutual dependence and mutual reinforcement. This brings me to my central question. What is it we can now do to nurture healthy, competent democracies, in old settings where democracy has grown weary and in new settings where it is freshly planted? I would make three suggestions, each of which is reflected in the experience of this university.

First, we must strengthen our civil institutions. This means realizing that a democratic society requires much more than democratic politics. Governments alone do not make democracy work. Private initiative is also essential, including a vital role for those institutions collectively described as civil society. By civil society I mean an array of institutions that operate on a private, voluntary basis but are driven by public motivations. They include institutions dedicated to education, to culture, to science and to research. They include commercial, labour, professional and ethnic associations, as well as entities devoted to maintaining health, protecting the environment and curing disease. Religious institutions are central to civil society, and so are institutions of the media. Sometimes, in our preoccupation with government and politics, we neglect the importance of civil institutions. I am not suggesting we ignore politics, but I am suggesting that we think beyond our political preoccupations. A thriving civil sector is essential in renewing the promise of democracy.

The second democratic pillar I would mention is education—rigorous, responsible and relevant education. We must do a better job of training leaders and shaping institutions to meet more demanding tests of competence and higher standards of excellence. This means moving beyond the notion that better education simply means broader schooling—wider access to formal learning. We must accompany our concern for quantity with a heightened concern for quality. Are the curricula we teach relevant to the knotty problems of the future? Or are we still providing a twentieth-century education for twenty-first-century leaders? Our Aga Khan Universities and Aga Khan Academies are addressing such questions as they work to advance the concept of meritocracy in the developing world and to maintain world-class standards that will stretch our students rather than patronizing them.

For too long some of our schools have taught too many subjects as subsets of dogmatic commitments. Economic insights, for example, were treated as ideological choices rather than as exercises in scientific problem solving. Too often, education made our students less flexible—confident to the point of arrogance that they now had all the answers—rather than more flexible—humble in their lifelong openness to new questions and new responses. An important goal of quality education is to equip each generation to participate effectively in what has been called "the great conversation" of our times. This means, on one hand, being unafraid of controversy. But, on the other hand, it also means being sensitive to the values and outlooks of others.

This brings me back to the current headlines. I must believe it is ignorance that explains the publishing of those caricatures that have brought such pain to Islamic peoples. I note that the Danish journal where the controversy originated acknowledged, in a recent letter of apology, that it had never realized the sensitivities involved. In this light, perhaps, the controversy can be described less as a clash of civilizations and more as a clash of ignorance. The alternative explanation would be that the offence was intended, in which case we would be confronted with evil of a different sort. But even to attribute the problem to ignorance is in no way to minimize its importance. In a pluralistic world, the consequences of ignorance can be profoundly damaging.

Perhaps, too, it is ignorance that has allowed so many participants in this discussion to confuse liberty with licence, implying that the sheer absence of restraint on human impulse can constitute a sufficient moral framework. This is not to say that governments should censor offensive speech. Nor does the answer lie in violent words or violent actions. But I am suggesting that freedom of expression is an incomplete value unless it is used honourably and that the obligations of citizenship in any society should include a commitment to informed and responsible expression. If we can commit ourselves, on all sides, to that objective, then the current crisis could become an educational opportunity—an occasion for enhanced awareness and broadened perspectives. Ignorance, arrogance, insensitivity—these attitudes rank high among the great public enemies of our time. The educational enterprise, at its best, can be an effective antidote to all of them.

Let me move, then, to my third suggestion for strengthening democracy in a pluralistic world—the renewal of ethical commitment. Democratic processes are presumably about the sharing of power, broadening the number who help shape social decisions. But that sharing, in and of itself, means little apart from the purposes for which power is finally used. To speak of end purposes, in turn, is to enter the realm of ethics. What are our ultimate goals? Whose interests do we seek to serve? How, in an increasingly cynical time, can we inspire people to a new set of aspirations, reaching beyond rampant materialism, the new relativism, self-serving individualism and resurgent tribalism? The search for justice and security, the struggle for equality of opportunity, the quest for tolerance and harmony, the pursuit of human dignity: these are moral imperatives we must work towards and think about daily.

In the ethical realm, as in the educational realm, one of the great stumbling blocks is arrogance. Even the resurgence of religious feeling, which should be such a positive force, can become a negative influence when it turns into self-righteousness. All of the world's great religions warn against this excess, yet in the name of those same religions too many are tempted to play God themselves rather than recognizing their humility before the Divine. A central element in a truly religious outlook, it seems to me, is the quality of personal humility—a recognition that, strive as we might, we will still fall short of our ideals; that, climb as we might, there will still be unexplored and mysterious peaks above us. It means recognizing our own creaturehood and thus our human limitations. In that recognition, it seems to me, lies our best protection against false prophecies and divisive dogmatism.

A deepening sense of spiritual commitment, and the ethical framework that goes with it, will be a central requirement if we are to find our way through the minefields and the quicksands of modern life. Strengthening religious institutions should be a vital part of this process. To be sure, freedom of religion is a critical value in a pluralistic society.

But if freedom of religion deteriorates into freedom from religion, then societies will find themselves lost in a bleak, unpromising landscape, with no compass, no road map and no sense of ultimate direction. What I am calling for, in sum, is an ethical sensibility that can be shared across denominational lines and can foster a universal moral outlook.

In conclusion, then, I would ask you to think with me about these three requirements: a new emphasis on civil institutions, a more rigorous concern for educational excellence and a renewed commitment to ethical standards. These are all ways in which we can encourage a climate of positive pluralism in our world and thus help to meet the current crisis of democracy. Only in such a climate will we come to see our differences as sources of enrichment rather than sources of division. And only in such a climate can we come to see "the other" not as a curse or a threat but as an opportunity and a blessing—whether "the other" lives across the street or across the world.

RENEWING DEMOCRACY'S PROMISE

SCHOOL *of* INTERNATIONAL *and*
PUBLIC AFFAIRS, COLUMBIA UNIVERSITY

New York, U.S.A., May 15, 2006

BISMILLAH-IR-RAHMAN-IR-RAHIM. An opinion poll reported recently that what American graduates want in a graduation speaker is "someone they can relate to." But that test, says the poll, showed the most popular university speaker in recent years was the Sesame Street character Kermit the Frog. I found it a bit intimidating to wonder just where the Imam of the Shia Ismaili Muslims would rank on the "relating" scale in comparison.

Ceremonies of the sort we observe today are valuable, because they help us to bridge the past and the future—to see ourselves as players in larger narratives. This school's narrative is now sixty years old, embracing the whole of the postwar period. In that time you have dramatically broadened both the communities you serve and the programs through which you serve them. Your history reflects a continuing conviction that the challenges of our times are fundamentally global ones, calling both for multidisciplinary and multinational responses.

Even as the School of International and Public Affairs marks its sixtieth anniversary, I am approaching an anniversary of my own—the fiftieth anniversary of my role as Imam of the Shia Imami Ismaili Muslims. Although I was educated in the West, my perspective over these fifty years has been profoundly shaped by the countries of South and Central Asia, the Middle East and Africa, where the Ismaili people live and where they are largely concentrated. For five decades, that has been my world—my virtually permanent preoccupation. And it is out of that experience that I speak today.

For the developing world, the past half-century has been a time of recurring hope and frequent disappointment. Great waves of change have washed over the landscape, from the crumbling of colonial hegemonies in mid-century to the recent collapse of Communist empires. But too often, what rushed in to replace the old order were empty hopes— not only the false allure of state socialism, non-alignment and single-party rule, but also the false glories of romantic nationalism and narrow tribalism, and the false dawn of runaway individualism.

There have been welcome exceptions to this pattern, of course. But too often, one step forward has been accompanied by two steps back. Hope for the future has often meant hope for survival, not hope for progress. The old order yielded its place, but a new world was not ready to be born. Today, this sense of frustration is compounded, in both rich and poor nations, by a host of new challenges. They range from changing weather patterns to mutating viruses, from new digital and biogenetic technologies to new patterns of family life and a new intermingling of cultures.

As the world economy integrates, global migrations are reaching record levels. Immigrants now account for two-thirds of the population growth in the thirty developed countries of the Organisation for Economic Co-operation and Development. Once homogenous societies are becoming distinctly multicultural. Meanwhile, the gap widens between rich countries and poor. Populations explode and the environment deteriorates. The nation state itself is newly challenged by the influence of non-state forces, including global crime and terrorism. Whenever I sit down with leading thinkers and policy makers, I come away with a haunting question. Why is it, given the scope of our collective learning—unprecedented in human history—that we have such difficulty in controlling these developments? Why is our growing intellectual mastery of the world so often accompanied in practice by a growing sense of drift?

My response to that question focusses increasingly on the fact that democratic institutions have not lived up to their potential. In both the developed and the developing world, the promise of democracy has too often been disappointed. For many centuries, enlightened people have argued that democracy was the key to social progress. But today, that contention is in dispute. In countries where I am directly involved, the twenty-first century has already experienced at least a half-dozen constitutional crises. The sad fact, hard to swallow and difficult to deny, is that nearly 40 per cent of UN member nations are now categorized not merely as failed states but as failed democracies. Our central challenge in this new century, as leaders and future leaders of our world, is to renew the democratic promise. The saving grace democratic systems are most likely to possess, after all, is that they are self-correcting. A system of public accountability still provides the best hope for change without violence. And that virtue alone redeems the entire concept. It explains Churchill's famous view that democracy is the worst form of government, except for all others. Our challenge is not to find alternatives to democracy but to find more and better ways to make democracy work.

In responding to that challenge today, I would like to make four observations—four suggestions for addressing our democratic disappointments and advancing our democratic hopes. My comments involve, first, the need for greater flexibility in defining the paths to democracy; second, the need for greater diversity in the institutions that participate in democratic life; third, the need to expand the public's capacity for democracy; and finally, the need to strengthen public integrity, on which democracy rests. Let me say a few words about each.

My first concern is that we must define the paths to democracy more flexibly. We like to say that democracy involves a pluralistic approach to life, but too seldom do we take a pluralistic approach to democracy. Too often, we insist that democracies must all follow a similar script, evolving at a similar pace, without recognizing that different circumstances may call for different constructs. The ultimate recourse in any democracy must be to the concept of popular sovereignty. But within that concept there is room for variation. One size need not fit all, and trying to make one size fit all can be a recipe for failure.

The world's most successful democracies have had widely differing histories, each taking its own shape according to its own timetable. How is power best divided and balanced? How should secular and spiritual allegiances interact? How can traditional authority—even monarchical authority—relate to democratic frameworks? How is the integrity of minority cultures and faith systems best reconciled with majority rule? It is simplistic to wish that our democratic destinations should be similar, that they cannot be reached by many paths. The democratic spirit of freedom and flexibility must begin with our definitions of democracy itself.

Even as we think more flexibly about democracy, we should also consider a second goal: diversifying the institutions of democratic life. One of the reasons governments often fail is that we depend too much on them. We invest too many hopes in political promises, and we entrust too many tasks to political regimes. Governments alone do not make democracy work. The most successful democracies are those in which the non-governmental institutions of civil society also play a vital role.

Civil society is powered by private voluntary energies, but it is committed to the public good. It includes institutions of education, health, science and research. It embraces professional, commercial, labour, ethnic and arts organizations, and others devoted to religion, communication and the environment. Sometimes, in our preoccupation with government, we discount the impact of civil society, including the potential of constructive NGOs. But we can no longer afford that outlook. Meeting the realities of a complex world will require a strengthened array of civic institutions. They spur social progress even when governments falter. And because they are so intimately connected to the public, they can predict new patterns and identify new problems with particular sensitivity.

But such developments cannot be coerced. They require an encouraging, enabling environment, supported by a broad public enthusiasm for social goals. And let me be clear: I am here because I believe your school, with its annual outpouring of able graduates, can make an enormous worldwide contribution to such a response. The development of civil society can also help meet the rising challenge of cultural diversity. As communities become more pluralistic in fact, they must also become more pluralistic in spirit. A vibrant civil society can give diverse constituencies effective ways to express and preserve their distinct identities, even as they interact with new neighbours.

We are often told that increased contact among cultures will inevitably produce a clash of civilizations, particularly between Islam and the West. Such predictions could become self-fulfilling prophecies if enough people believe them. But that need not, and must not, be the case. The true problem we face is what I would call a clash of ignorance on both sides—one that neglects, for example, a long history of respect and cooperation between Islamic and Western peoples and their respective civilizations. This is an appropriate place to recall how North American history was shaped over the centuries by diverse cultural groups. In the future as in the past, such diversity can be an engine of enormous creativity if it is sustained by what I would call a new cosmopolitan ethic. To encourage that process, the Aga Khan Development Network has recently formed a partnership with the Government of Canada to create a new Global Centre for Pluralism in Ottawa. Drawing on both the Ismaili experience and the pluralistic model of Canada itself, the Centre recognizes that we cannot make the world safe for democracy unless we also make the world safe for diversity and that the institutions of civil society can contribute significantly to that goal.

My third point involves the public capacity for democratic government. This is a problem we often treat with too much sentimentality, reluctant to acknowledge that democratic publics are not always all-wise. Inadequate public communication is part of the problem. Driven by short-term circulation and profit goals, media increasingly tell audiences what they want to hear rather than what they ought to hear. And what too many people want is not to be informed but to be entertained. One result is the inadequacy of international news. I am told that world news now represents a substantially lower percentage of mainstream American news than it did a generation ago. Thanks to the Internet, specialists can get more information from more places than ever before. But for the general public, in America and elsewhere, global information has declined, while global involvements have expanded.

If better communication is one part of the answer, better education is another. This means, above all, developing new curricula to meet new demands, especially in developing countries. We must do more to prepare the leaders of the twenty-first century for economic life in a global marketplace, for cultural life in pluralistic societies, for political life in complex democracies. Our system of Aga Khan–sponsored universities and academies is working throughout the developing world to create new educational models. But the scale of our work only begins to address the enormity of the challenge.

Improved communication and education can be helpful, but we also must be realistic about public capabilities. I believe, for example, that publics are too often asked to vote on issues that bewilder them. In recent months, both in Africa and in Asia, new national constitutions have been left to the mercies of mass public referenda, posing complex, theoretical issues well beyond the ability of politicians to explain and publics to master. Nor is this matter unique to the developing world. We saw a similar pattern in 2005 when the French public rejected a new European constitutional treaty that was 474 pages long. Democracies need to distinguish responsibly between the prerogatives of the people and the obligations of their leaders. And leaders must meet their obligations. When democracies fail, it is usually because publics have grown impatient with ineffectual leaders and governments.

When parliaments lack the structure or the expertise to grapple with complex problems, or when a system of checks and balances stymies action rather than refining it, then disenchanted publics will often turn to autocrats. The UN Development Program recently reported, for example, that 55 per cent of those surveyed in eighteen Latin American countries would support authoritarian rule if it brought economic progress. There, in too many cases, progress and democracy have not gone hand in hand.

The best way to redeem the concept of democracy around the world is to improve the results it delivers. Developed countries, rather than talking so much about democracy on the conceptual level, must·do more—much more—to help democracy work on a practical level. Our goal must be fully functioning democracies that bring genuine improvements in the quality of life for their peoples. We must not force publics to choose between democratic government and competent government.

This brings me to my final topic: the need for a sense of greater public integrity. Expanding the number of people who share social power is only half the battle. The critical question is how such power is used. How can we inspire people to reach beyond rampant materialism, self-indulgent individualism and unprincipled relativism? One answer is to augment our focus on personal prerogatives and individual rights, with an expanded concern for personal responsibilities and communal goals. A passion for justice, the quest for equality, a respect for tolerance, a dedication to human dignity: these are universal human values broadly shared across divisions of class, race, language, faith and geography. They constitute what classical philosophers in the East and West alike have described as human virtue—not merely the absence of negative restraints on individual freedom, but also a set of positive responsibilities, moral disciplines that prevent liberty from turning into licence.

Historically, one of the most powerful resources for any culture has been the sense that it is heading somewhere, that tomorrow will be better than today, that there is reason to embrace what I would call a narrative of progress. The right of individuals to look for a better quality of life within their own lifespans and to build towards a better life for their children: these are personal aspirations that must become public values. But a healthy sense of public integrity, in my view, will be difficult to nurture over time without a strong religious underpinning. In the Islamic tradition, the conduct of one's worldly life is inseparably intertwined with the concerns of one's spiritual life. One cannot talk about integrity without also talking about faith. For Islam, the importance of this intersection is an item of faith, such a profound melding of worldly concerns and spiritual ideals that one cannot imagine one without the other. The two belong together. They constitute a way of life. From that perspective, I would put high among our priorities, both within and outside the Islamic world, the need to renew our spiritual traditions. To be sure, religious freedom is a critical value in a pluralistic society. But if freedom of religion deteriorates into freedom from religion, then I fear we will soon be lost on a bleak and barren landscape with no compass or road map, no sense of ultimate direction.

I fully understand the West's historical commitment to separating the secular from the religious. But for many non-Westerners, including most Muslims, the realms of faith and worldly affairs cannot be antithetical. If modernism lacks a spiritual dimension, it will look like materialism. And if the modernizing influence of the West is insistently and exclusively a secularizing influence, then much of the Islamic world will be somewhat distanced from it.

A deeply rooted sense of public integrity means more than integrity in government, important as that must be. Ethical lapses in medicine and education, malfeasance in business and banking, dishonesty among journalists, scientists, engineers or scholars—all of these weaknesses can undermine the most promising democracies.

Let me finally emphasize my strong conviction that public integrity cannot grow out of authoritarian pronouncements. It must be rooted in the human heart and conscience. As the Holy Quran says, "There is no compulsion in religion." The resurgence of spirituality, potentially such a positive force, can become a negative influence when it turns into self-righteousness and imposes itself on others. Like all of the world's great religions, Islam warns against the danger of comparing oneself with God and places primary emphasis on the qualities of generosity, mercy and humility. A central element in any religious outlook, it seems to me, is a sense of human limitation, a recognition of our own creaturehood—a posture of profound humility before the Divine. In that sensibility lies our best protection against divisive dogmatism and our best hope for creative pluralism.

In conclusion, then, I would ask, as you move out from this university into a diverse and demanding world, that you think about four considerations for renewing the promise of democracy: defining democratic paths more flexibly; expanding the role of civil society; increasing public capacities for self-governance; and strengthening our commitment to public integrity. In all these ways, I believe we can help restore confidence in the promise of democratic life, affirming with pride our distinct cultural identities while embracing with enthusiasm our new global potentials. To the graduates, my prayer is that God may guide you and accompany you as you fulfill your destinies.

THE SPIRITUAL ROOTS OF TOLERANCE

TUTZING EVANGELICAL ACADEMY,
UPON RECEIVING *the* TOLERANCE PRIZE

Tutzing, Germany, May 20, 2006

B ISMILLAH-IR-RAHMAN-IR-RAHIM. I would like to take this occasion, at the opening of these comments, to tell Minister Steinmeier how much all the people who work with me around the world appreciate the support and partnership of the people and the government of Germany in the work we are doing. You have brought imagination, you have brought sophistication, you have brought flexibility to areas of need, areas of intellectual activity, that we consider unique, and I thank you for that. In these times of misunderstanding and mistrust, I applaud the realistic outlook on international affairs that His Excellency the Minister of Foreign Affairs brings to his work. I know he views a constructive relationship between the West and the Muslim world as critical to global peace and stability, and I am grateful for his contributions to that goal.

I am also deeply grateful for your kind invitation and your generous award. This honour takes on special distinction for me because of the very high value I attach to the award's purpose: to increase awareness and respect among peoples and cultures through a discussion of political, cultural and religious topics. It is to these subjects that I will address my comments today.

In doing so, I would like to draw on my personal experience, as one who was educated in the West but has spent nearly fifty years working largely in the developing world. My particular preoccupation during this time has been with the countries of South and Central Asia, Africa and the Middle East, where the Ismaili community is concentrated.

Since I became Imam of the Shia Imami Ismaili Muslims, I have watched my world—or should I say the entire world?—oscillate between promise and disappointment. In many cases, the disappointments can be attributed to the absence of a culture of tolerance. Of course my experience includes the religious faith in which I have been nurtured. I was born into a Muslim family and educated as a Muslim, and I have spent many years studying the history of the faith and its civilizations. My commitment to the principle of tolerance also grows out of that commitment.

One of the central elements of the Islamic faith is the inseparable nature of faith and world. The two are so deeply intertwined that one cannot imagine their separation. They constitute a "way of life." The role and responsibility of an Imam, therefore, is both to interpret the faith to the community and also to do all within his means to improve the quality and security of people's daily lives. I am fascinated and somewhat frustrated when representatives of the Western world, especially the Western media, try to describe the work of our Aga Khan Development Network in fields like education, health, the economy, media and the building of social infrastructure. Reflecting a certain historical tendency of the West to separate the secular from the religious, they often describe it either as philanthropy or entrepreneurship. What is not understood is that this work is, for us, a part of our institutional responsibility. It flows from the mandate of the office of Imam to improve the quality of worldly life for the concerned communities.

Our spiritual understandings, like those of your academy, are rooted in ancient teachings. In the case of Islam, there are two touchstones I have long treasured and sought to apply. The first affirms the unity of the human race, as expressed in the Holy Quran where God, as revealed through the Holy Prophet Muhammad (may peace be upon him) says the following: "O mankind! Be careful of your duty to your Lord, Who created you from a single soul and from it created its mate and from the twain hath spread abroad a multitude of men and women." (4:1) This remarkable verse speaks both of the inherent diversity of mankind—the multitude—and of the unity of humankind—the single soul created by a single Creator—a spiritual legacy that distinguishes the human race from all other forms of life.

The second passage I would cite today is from the first hereditary Imam of the Shia community, Hazrat Ali. As you know, the Shia divided from the Sunni after the death of the Prophet Muhammad (peace be upon him). Hazrat Ali, the cousin and son-in-law of the Prophet, was, in Shia belief, named by the Prophet to be the Legitimate Authority for the interpretation of the faith. For the Shia today, all over the world, he is regarded as the first Imam.

I cite Hazrat Ali's words so that you may understand the spirit in which I have attempted to fulfill the mandate left to me as the forty-ninth hereditary Ismaili Imam after the death of my grandfather. I quote: "No belief is like modesty and patience, no attainment is like humility, no honour is like knowledge, no power is like forbearance, and no support is more reliable than consultation." Hazrat Ali's regard for knowledge reinforces the compatibility of faith and the world. And his respect for consultation is, in my view, a commitment to tolerant and open-hearted democratic processes.

These Islamic ideals, of course, have also been emphasized by other great religions. Despite the long history of religious conflict, there is a long counter-history of religious focus on tolerance as a central virtue—on welcoming the stranger and loving one's neighbour. "Who is my neighbour?" one of the central Christian narratives asks. Jesus responds by telling the story of the Good Samaritan—a foreigner, a representative of the Other, who reaches out sympathetically, across ethnic and cultural divides, to show mercy to the fallen stranger at the side of the road.

I know you will find nothing unusual in this discussion given your own spiritual foundations. But it is striking to me how many modern thinkers are still disposed to link tolerance with secularism and religion with intolerance. In their eyes—and often in the public's eyes, I fear—religion is seen as part of the problem and not part of the solution. To be sure, there are reasons why this impression exists. Throughout history, we find terrible chapters in which religious conflict brought frightening results. Sometimes, part of the problem grew from proselytizing, in which faith was not so much shared as imposed. Again in our day, many ostensibly religious voices aggressively affirm a single faith by denying or condemning others.

When people speak these days about an inevitable clash of civilizations in our world, what they often mean, I fear, is an inevitable clash of religions. But I would use different terminology altogether. The essential problem, as I see it, in relations between the Muslim world and the West is a clash of ignorance. And what I would prescribe as an essential first step is a concentrated educational effort. Instead of shouting at one another, we must listen to one another and learn from one another. As we do, one of our first lessons might well centre on those powerful but often neglected chapters in history when Islamic and European cultures interacted cooperatively—constructively and creatively—to help realize some of civilization's peak achievements.

We must also understand the vast diversity within individual faiths and cultures, including the diversity now at play within the Islamic world. And we must acknowledge that although such pluralism can be healthy and enriching, it can also become destructive and deadly, as it did for the Christian community in Europe half a millennium ago and it does in some parts of the Islamic world at the start of this new millennium. Intolerance can thus result from one sort of presumably religious attitude, but profound tolerance can also be a deeply religious commitment.

The spiritual roots of tolerance include, it seems to me, a respect for individual conscience, seen as a gift of God, as well as a posture of religious humility before the Divine. It is by accepting our human limits that we come to see the Other as a fellow seeker of truth and to find common ground in our common quest. Let me emphasize again, however, that spirituality should not become a way of escaping from the world but rather a way of more actively engaging in it. There are a variety of ways in which we can work to build a culture of tolerance in a turbulent time. Many of them are reflected in the work of our Aga Khan Development Network. One example is the new Global Centre for Pluralism, which we recently established in Ottawa, in partnership with the Canadian government. The Centre sees the minority experience of the Ismaili community as a helpful resource in the quest for a constructive pluralism, along with the pluralistic model of Canada itself.

The challenges to tolerance are manifold, in both the developed and the developing world. The revolutionary impact of globalization means that many who never met before now intermingle continually, through modern communications media and through direct contact. The migration of populations around the world is at record levels; peoples who once lived across the world from one another now live across the street. But societies that have grown more pluralistic in makeup are not always growing more pluralistic in spirit. What is needed, all across the world, is a new cosmopolitan ethic rooted in a strong culture of tolerance.

I recall a conversation I had some years ago with Jim Wolfensohn, then president of the World Bank, about perceptions of happiness in various societies, especially among the very poor. We decided that we should listen to the voices of the poor, and the World Bank commissioned an important study on that topic. One of its conclusions was that the emotion of fear was a central factor holding these societies back. Such fear could have many forms: fear of tyrants; fear of nature; fear of ill health; fear of corruption, violence, scarcity and impoverishment. And such fears inevitably became a source of intolerance.

There is a human impulse, it seems, fed by fear, to define identity in negative terms. We often determine who we are by determining who we are against. This fragmenting impulse not only separates peoples from one another, but it also subdivides communities, and then it subdivides the subdivisions. It leads to what some have called the fraying of society, in which communities come to resemble a worn-out cloth as a tight weave separates into individual strands. But the human inclination to divisiveness is accompanied, I deeply believe, by a profound human impulse to bridge divisions. And often the more secure we are in our own identities, the more effective we can be in reaching out to others. If our animosities are born out of fear, then confident generosity is born out of hope. One of the central lessons I have learned after a half century of working in the developing world is that the replacement of fear by hope is probably the single most powerful trampoline of progress. Even in the poorest and most isolated communities, we have found that decades, if not centuries, of angry conflict can be turned around by giving people reasons to work together towards a better future—in other words, by giving them reasons to hope. And when hope takes root, then a new level of tolerance is possible, although it may have been unknown for years and years and years.

Tolerance that grows out of hope is more than a negative virtue, more than a convenient way to ease sectarian tensions or foster social stability, more than a sense of forbearance when the views of others clash with our own. Instead, seen not as a pallid religious compromise but as a sacred religious imperative, tolerance can become a powerful, positive force—one that allows all of us to expand our horizons and enrich our lives.

TOWARDS A COMMON FUTURE

SIGNING CEREMONY *for the*
GLOBAL CENTRE *for* PLURALISM

Ottawa, Canada, October 25, 2006

BISMILLAH-IR-RAHMAN-IR-RAHIM. It was just eighteen months ago that the Government of Canada announced its decision to partner with the Ismaili Imamat and the Aga Khan Development Network in our Global Centre for Pluralism. What we welcomed at that time was a multifaceted partnership—financial, yes, but also institutional and intellectual.

Our sense of partnership is not a new development. In fact, the AKDN and Canada have built a unique collaboration over nearly a quarter-century on a wide variety of projects in a wide variety of places, especially South and Central Asia, East and West Africa, and the Middle East. We have a long history of path-breaking cooperation. This successful collaboration, moreover, is deeply rooted in a remarkable convergence of values—our strong mutual dedication to the concept and practice of pluralism.

In my own role as Imam of the Shia Ismaili Muslims over the past half-century, I have come to appreciate the importance of pluralism in ever-expanding ways. The Ismaili community, after all, is itself a global family, spanning many geographies, cultures, languages and ethnicities, and sharing its life with people of many faiths. In addition, much of my work over this time has dealt with highly diverse societies in the developing world, often suffering from poverty, violence and despair. In such circumstances, a commitment to pluralism comes as no accident. For pluralism, in essence, is a deliberate set of choices that a society must make if it is to avoid costly conflict and harness the power of its diversity in solving human problems.

It will not surprise you that I am fascinated by Canada's experience as a successful pluralistic society. My active engagement with Canada began in the 1970s, when many Ismailis found a welcoming refuge here from East African ethnic strife. Since that time, the Ismaili community has planted deep roots here and become self-sufficient, and it can now make its own contributions to Canada's pluralistic model. That model, in turn, is one that can help to teach and inspire the entire world.

Comme les Canadiens le savent si bien, l'idéal du pluralisme n'est pas nouveau en ce monde. Il a des fondations honorables et anciennes, y compris des racines profondes dans la tradition islamique. Ce qui est sans précédent aujourd'hui, c'est une société mondialisée, intimement interconnectée et extraordinairement interdépendante. De nombreux facteurs ont contribué à ce nouvel ordre: la fin de la Guerre froide, les avancées techniques des transports et des communications, les migrations accélérées des peuples. Or l'impact de ces forces va probablement s'intensifier à l'avenir. À mon avis, ce à quoi nous faisons face actuellement, c'est à une nouvelle et éprouvante période de l'histoire humaine, où les valeurs et les pratiques pluralistes séculaires ne sont plus tout simplement désirables—elles sont devenues absolument essentielles—et pas seulement pour l'évolution future du monde mais également pour notre survie même.

The Ismaili Imamat and the Aga Khan Development Network are deeply grateful to the government and the people of Canada for the continuing spirit of vision, generosity and mutual respect that has brought us to this landmark moment.

Indeed, our agreement itself exemplifies pluralism at work. It brings together people, ideas and resources from different continents and cultures, from religious and secular traditions, and from the public and the private sectors. The sense of momentum we feel at this hour will surely give us renewed confidence as we seek to connect our diversified pasts with our common future. Our hope and expectation is that the Global Centre for Pluralism will become a vital force in our world for research, learning and dialogue, engaging Canadians from all walks of life and linking a widening array of partners. I am grateful that the Government of Canada has contributed so generously to its material and intellectual resources. Making available the old war museum is a particularly generous and symbolic gesture. Let us replace war with peace. Our own commitment is to invest in this building so that it becomes a worthy testament to Canada's global leadership in the cause of pluralism.

Those who talk about an inevitable "clash of civilizations" can point today to an accumulating array of symptoms that sometimes seem to reflect their diagnosis. I believe, however, that this diagnosis is wrong—that these symptoms are more dramatic than they are representative and that they are rooted in human ignorance rather than in human character. The problem of ignorance is a problem that can be addressed. Perhaps it can even be ameliorated, but only if we go to work on our educational tasks with sustained energy, creativity and intelligence.

That is why we felt the Global Centre for Pluralism was needed. That is why the Global Centre for Pluralism exists today. And that is why the Global Centre for Pluralism holds such enormous promise for all of our tomorrows.

"PLURALISM IS A WORK IN PROGRESS"

THIS CONVERSATION BETWEEN HIS
HIGHNESS *the* AGA KHAN *and*
PETER MANSBRIDGE, HOST *of* CBC
TELEVISION'S *MANSBRIDGE
ONE ON ONE*, ORIGINALLY AIRED ON
OCTOBER 28 *and* 29, 2006.

PETER MANSBRIDGE: You must love Canada—you keep coming back here.

HIS HIGHNESS THE AGA KHAN: I do.

PM: What is the quality that you most admire about this country?

AK: I think a number of qualities. First of all, a pluralist society that has invested in building pluralism, where communities from all different backgrounds and faiths are happy. A modern country that deals with modern issues, not running away from them but dealing with the tough ones. And a global commitment to values, Canadian values, which I think are very important.

PM: I wonder whether your confidence in Canada has in any way been shattered in these past few years, especially since 9/11. There have been tensions in this country, as in many other Western countries, between the Muslim and the non-Muslim societies on any number of levels, on both sides, about history and religion and tradition and integration within society. How much has that concerned you?

AK: It concerns me, and at the same time it doesn't. To me, building and sustaining a pluralist society is always going to be a work in progress. It doesn't have a finite end, and so long as there is national intent, civic intent to make pluralism work, then one accepts that it's a work in progress.

PM: Let me go a little deeper on that, because it raises a question you have often raised: the issue of ignorance. You reject the theory of a clash of civilizations, or even a clash of religions. You believe there's a clash of ignorance here, on both sides of the divide, and you've felt that way for a long time. I was looking through transcripts of an interview you gave in the 1980s in Canada in which you were warning the West that it had to do a better job in trying to understand Islam. That clearly hasn't happened.

AK: No, it hasn't happened. A number of friends and people in important places have tried to contribute to solving that problem, but it's a long-established problem, and it's going to take, I think, several decades before we reach a situation where the definition of an educated person includes a basic understanding of the Islamic world. That hasn't been the case, and the absence of that basic education has caused all sorts of misunderstandings, above all the inability to predict. Statehood, international affairs, economic affairs are often predicated on the ability to predict. If you don't know the issues and the forces at play, the ability to predict is severely constrained.

PM: What's been the resistance, do you think?

AK: I think it's essentially historic. Judeo-Christian societies have developed their own education over decades and more, and basic knowledge of the Islamic world has simply been absent. If you look at what was required in education in the 1980s, for example—I was a student in the U.S.—basic education on the Islamic world was absent, even in general courses on the humanities, for example.

PM: Is this a one-sided clash of ignorance?

AK: No, I think there is ignorance on both sides, and very often there is confusion. I think, more and more, there has been confusion between, for example, religion and civilization. And that's introducing instability into the discussion, frankly. I would prefer to talk about ignorance regarding the civilizations of the Islamic world rather than just ignorance about the faith of Islam.

PM: What we've witnessed in the last couple of years, not just in this country but in other Western countries as well, is what we call homegrown terror, where you see young Muslim men, educated in the West, who are moving towards a fundamentalist view, a militant view of Islam. Why is that happening?

AK: There is, without any doubt, a growing sense amongst Muslim communities around the world that there are forces at play they don't control but that view the Muslim world with—let's say unhappiness, or more. I would simply say, however, that if you analyze the situation, I don't think you can conclude that all Muslims from all backgrounds are part of that phenomenon. Second, if you go back and look at it, you will find in a lot of those communities a long-standing, unresolved political crisis. It's very, very risky, I think, to interpret these situations as being specific to the faith of Islam. It is specific to peoples, sometimes ethnic groups, but it's not specific to the faith of Islam.

PM: That must really concern you. Your followers believe in you, see you as a direct descendant of the Prophet Muhammad, the same Prophet that some of these minority fundamentalist militant groups hold up and claim as the reason for their actions.

AK: Again, I think one has to go back and say, what is the cause of this situation? With all due respect, if you look at the crisis in the Middle East, that crisis was born at the end of the First World War. The crisis in Kashmir was born through the freedom of the Indian continent. These are political issues originally; they are not religious issues. You can't attribute the faith of Islam to them. The second point I would make is this tendency to generalize Islam. There are many different interpretations of Islam. As a Muslim, if I said to you that I didn't recognize the difference between a Greek Orthodox and a Russian Orthodox or a Protestant and a Catholic, I think you'd say to me, "But you don't understand the Christian world." Well, let me reverse that question.

PM: Canada's role in Afghanistan is well known and has been since 9/11. So is that of the Aga Khan Foundation, which is in Afghanistan in a big way in development matters. The question is simple, really. With all the help that has been given to Afghanistan, why is the Taliban resurging, not only back in numbers but back in some sense in popularity?

AK: I think there are a number of reasons, but the one I would put forward as the most immediate is the slow process of reconstruction. There was a lot of hope that once there was regime change and a new government, and a political process had been completed, etc., people's quality of life would change, and it hasn't changed quickly enough. It's taken much more time than many of us had hoped to get to isolated communities in Afghanistan and improve their quality of life. It's an organizational problem. Even amongst the donor countries, there have been differences of opinion, and the management of the drug problem has not been a united effort by any means. So there are a number of things that have slowed up the process. And there are still acute pockets of poverty in Afghanistan. People don't have enough food, people don't have access to any education, any health care, and it is clear this sort of frustration causes bitterness and a search for other solutions.

PM: Well, is there time to turn it around, because you get a sense that the pendulum has swung back considerably in the last year or so. You're friends with Hamid Karzai, the president of Afghanistan, and I have talked to him a couple of times in the last few years. There is a growing sense amongst the Canadian people as well of frustration and a belief that it's a war that cannot be won.

AK: I would beg to differ on that. I think what we are seeing in Afghanistan, at least from my own network of activities, is an increasingly visible two-speed process. In the north and the west of the country, you are beginning to see quantifiable change. In the east and the south, you're not seeing that. That two-speed change is going to have to be managed with great care, but it's not a good reason to give up, by any means.

PM: Can you do both at the same time—that's the debate in Canada—run a military operation, I'm talking specifically about the south, while trying to introduce aid and development in an area that is not secure?

AK: Very difficult to do, but necessary. Every step counts. Certainly in areas where there is insecurity, I think the ability of populations to participate in these sorts of activities does go down when quality of life changes. I believe the same thing with regard to the drug problem.

PM: How much of the problem in Afghanistan is a result of the decision on the part of the Americans and the British to move into Iraq?

AK: Very substantial indeed. The invasion of Iraq was something that has mobilized what we call the Ummah, the community of Muslims around the world. Every Muslim I have ever talked to has felt engaged by this.

PM: On what level?

AK: Well, Baghdad is one of the great historic cities of the Islamic world. Iraq is not a new country, it is part of the history of our civilization. It has been a pluralist country, with great philosophers, great historians, great scientists. Reverse the question again. What would the Christian world think if a Muslim army attacked Rome? I think there would be a general reaction in the Christian world, not just an Italian reaction.

PM: But it seems even in the Muslim world that invasion has caused major divisions, the clash within Islam itself, between Shia and Sunni.

AK: That was entirely predictable. Entirely predictable. What you were effectively doing was placing a Sunni minority government in a country that had a Shia demographic majority. And again, take the case out of its situation. What would happen—I'm sorry to come back to this, but it's important—if a Muslim army went into Northern Ireland and replaced one Christian interpretation with another? Imagine the fallout that would cause in the Christian world itself.

PM: So what happens now? Can Iraq be put back together? And who would be doing that?

AK: That's a very, very difficult question. I would not want to predict the answer, because I think that the whole process of change in Iraq has regional dimensions that have got to be managed. They are not just national dimensions in Iraq. Those regional dimensions also were predictable, let's be quite frank about it, and I think they are going to have to be managed with very, very great care.

PM: Is the answer, as some suggest, the splitting of the country into three regions, with the main two combatants, the Shia and the Sunni, actually separated by borders?

AK: That's really an issue where the leaders of the three communities have got to agree or not. In my life, in the past fifty years, I have been uncomfortable with the creation of unviable states. So I would ask the question: if you did do that, what components of Iraq would be stable, viable states in the future?

PM: Who's showing leadership in the world right now, in terms of the major global issues? Who do you look to as a leader?

AK: There are a number of people in THE UN system who have shown leadership, who have shown balanced judgment on these issues. Because when all is said and done, it is the balance of the judgment that counts, and it is understanding the issues. Amongst others, Kofi Annan has been remarkable in his understanding of the issues. He's also had a team of people around him who are very good.

PM: It's quite a condemnation of the political leaders of our generation that you don't point to one of them, no matter which side they are on of the divide we talked of earlier. You don't see anyone there?

AK: I'm looking more in terms of the regions of Africa, Central Asia, and I'm asking myself, within these contexts, who is having the greatest influence? Certainly the UN, UNDP [United Nations Development Programme], I think the World Bank under Jim Wolfensohn changed direction very significantly and dealt with real human issues and has done a wonderful job.

PM: Some people suggest that there's been a movement away, in terms of real leadership, from governments to private foundations, philanthropic organizations, yours being one. The Gates Foundation, and you can name a number; for example, Bono, the singer. Do you see that happening, and is that a good thing?

AK: I see it happening and I welcome it wholeheartedly, because what we are talking about, I think, is accelerating the construction of civil society. I personally think that civil society is one of the most urgent things to build around the world. One of the phenomena you see today is that, in a number of countries where governments have been unstable, etc., progress has continued when there has been a strong civil society. And that's a lesson that I think all of us have to learn. My own network is immensely committed to that. What the Gates Foundation and others are doing is providing new resources, new thoughts to create civil society, whether it is in health care or education. It is the combined input that is so exciting and so important.

PM: A new Global Centre for Pluralism will be established here in Canada through the Aga Khan Foundation and the Government of Canada. What is your hope for that? What do you see that accomplishing?

AK: I hope that this Centre will learn from the Canadian history of pluralism, the bumpy road that all societies must travel in dealing with pluralist problems and the outcomes. That can offer much of the world new thoughts, new ways of dealing with issues, anticipating the problems that can occur. In recent years, I think, we are seeing more and more around the world, no matter what the nature of the conflict is, that ultimately there is a rejection of pluralism as one of the components, whether it is tribalism, whether it is conflict amongst ethnic groups, whether it is conflict amongst religions. The failure to see value in pluralism is a terrible liability.

PM: Why Canada?

AK: Because I think Canada is a country that is invested in making this potential liability become an asset. Canada has been, perhaps, too humble in its own appreciation of this global asset. Few countries, if any, have been as successful as Canada has, bumpy though the road is. As I said earlier, it is always going to be an unfinished task.

PM: In 2007 you will mark your Golden Jubilee, fifty years. I was going to ask, what's your dream for the world, but I guess dreams are dreams. What's your realistic hope?

AK: Well, clearly, I would like to see the areas of the world that are living in horrible poverty, I'd like to see that replaced by an environment where people can live in more hope than they have had. I would like to see governments produce enabling environments where society can function and grow, rather than live in the dogmatisms that we've all lived through and that, I think, have been very constraining. And I'd like to see solid institutional building, because when all is said and done societies need institutional capacity.

PM: Well, these are grand hopes. I'm sure they are shared by many. How realistic do you think it is that we can achieve anything like this?

AK: I think we can achieve a lot of that. I think the time frame is what we don't control. I remember in the mid-1950s reading about countries in the developing world being referred to as "basket cases." Fifty years later, these are some of the most powerful countries in the world. They have enormous populations, but they are exporting food, when fifty years ago we were told they would never be able to feed themselves. They had an incredible technology deficit fifty years ago. Today they are exporting technology, homegrown technology. So I think there are a number of cases out there where we can say, what we don't control is the time factor, but society does have the capability to make those changes.

PM: So there is reason for hope?

AK: I believe so, God willing.

HIS HIGHNESS THE Aga Khan became Imam (spiritual leader) of the Shia Imami Ismaili Muslims on July 11, 1957, at the age of twenty, succeeding his grandfather, Sir Sultan Mahomed Shah Aga Khan. He is the forty-ninth hereditary Imam of the Shia Imami Ismaili Muslims and a direct descendant of the Prophet Muhammad (peace be upon him) through the Prophet's cousin and son-in-law, Hazrat Ali, the first Imam, and Ali's wife Fatima, the Prophet's daughter.

Today, Ismailis live in twenty-five countries, mainly in South and Central Asia, East Africa, the Middle East, Europe and North America. Over the five decades since the present Aga Khan became Imam, there have been major political and economic changes in most of these areas, including independence from colonialism in South Asia and Africa and the collapse of the Soviet Union. Canada is home to a significant number of Ismailis, many of whom arrived as refugees following the ethnic strife in East Africa in the 1970s.

The Aga Khan emphasizes Islam as a thinking, spiritual faith: one that teaches compassion, embraces pluralism and upholds the dignity of human beings. In the Shia tradition, it is the mandate of the Imam to give practical expression to the social conscience of Islam. For the Aga Khan, promoting the development of all people, irrespective of their faith, is not a matter of philanthropy but rather a duty of the office he holds.

In consonance with this vision of Islam and the Ismaili tradition of service to humanity, the Aga Khan conceived and founded the Aga Khan Development Network, a group of institutions working to improve living conditions and opportunities in specific regions of the developing world. In every country, these institutions work for the common good of all citizens regardless of their faith, origin or gender.

The integrated agencies that form the AKDN have mandates ranging from health and education to architecture, culture, microfinance, disaster mitigation, rural development, the promotion of private-sector enterprise and the revitalization of historic cities. They include the Aga Khan Foundation, Aga Khan Health Services, Aga Khan Education Services, the Aga Khan Agency for Microfinance, Aga Khan Planning and Building Services, Focus Humanitarian Assistance, the Aga Khan Trust for Culture, the University of Central Asia, Aga Khan University and the Aga Khan Fund for Economic Development. Together, these institutions constitute one of the largest development entities in the world.

Canada and the AKDN have forged a unique partnership through twenty-five years of fruitful and diverse collaboration, beginning with the Canadian government's support of the Aga

Khan Rural Support Programme in Northern Pakistan. The World Partnership Walk, an initiative of Aga Khan Foundation Canada, is the country's largest annual event in support of international cooperation. Aga Khan has recently announced four new initiatives in Canada: the Global Centre for Pluralism and the Delegation of the Ismaili Imamat in Ottawa, and the Ismaili Centre and the Aga Khan Museum in Toronto. These represent an exciting agenda of future collaboration that will draw on the complementarities of the Imamat and Canada and strengthen Canada's contribution to global peace and development.

The Aga Khan Development Network
P.O. Box 2049
1–3 Avenue de la Paix
1211 Geneva 2, Switzerland
Tel. (+41 22) 909 7200
Fax (+41 22) 909 7292
www.akdn.org

Aga Khan Foundation Canada
360 Albert Street, Suite 1220
Ottawa, Ontario   K1R 7X7
Tel. (613) 237-2532
Fax (613) 567-2532
www.akfc.ca

HIS HIGHNESS THE AGA KHAN is the forty-ninth hereditary Imam of the Shia Ismaili Muslims. He assumed the office of the Imamat in July 1957, making 2007 the Golden Jubilee of his spiritual leadership. During that time he has worked on an international scale to improve living conditions and foster social, cultural and economic opportunities for men and women in the developing world. The Aga Khan Development Network, which he established in 1980, encompasses foundations, universities and programs in thirty countries, including Aga Khan Foundation Canada. One of the Aga Khan Development Network's recent projects is the Global Centre for Pluralism, which is being established in Ottawa in cooperation with the Government of Canada.

His Highness the Aga Khan has received numerous awards, distinctions and honorary doctorates for his service to humanity. In 2005, he was invested as an honorary Companion of the Order of Canada in recognition of a lifetime of outstanding achievement, dedication to the community and service to the nation.